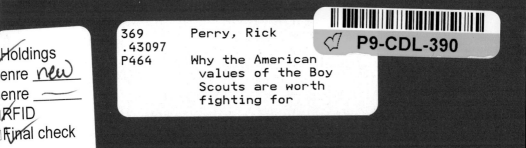

ON MY HONOR

Why the American Values of the Boy Scouts Are Worth Fighting For

Rick Perry,
Governor

Stroud & Hall Publishers
P.O. Box 27210
Macon, Ga 31221
www.stroudhall.com

The paper used in this publication meets the minimum requirements
of American National Standard for Information Sciences—
Permanence of Paper for Printed Library Materials.
ANSI Z39.48–1984. (alk. paper)

Library of Congress Cataloging-in-Publication Data

Perry, Rick, 1950–
Why the American values of the Boy Scouts are worth fighting for / by Rick Perry.
p. cm.
Includes bibliographical references and index.
ISBN 978-0-9796462-2-5 (alk. paper)
1. Boy Scouts of America. 2. Social values—United States. I. Title.

HS3313.P47 2008
369.430973—dc22
2007040683

From Boy Scout to Eagle Scout to governor of one of the largest states in the union—who better to tell the story of one of our country's greatest institutions? Governor Perry pulls no punches as he details the relentless assault on the Scouts and the traditional American values they instill. It's an important read for anyone concerned about the battle over how our children are raised.

—Sean Hannity

"Governor Perry's book, *On My Honor*, defends the values espoused by an organization that has been instrumental in supporting the American family: the Boy Scouts of America. It dives deep into the culture war, showing how the proponents of secularism have transformed the virtue of liberty into the vice of license. Perry makes a passionate defense for Scouting, recognizing how valuable this movement has been in setting young men on a course to achievement. When you consider that the American family is under siege, we need organizations like the Boy Scouts of America to not only survive, but thrive, in building stronger communities. This great organization has helped thousands of single mothers raise young boys to live according to the American ethic, and many more parents build a stronger bond with their children centered on wholesome activities that edify the family. I applaud Governor Perry for standing up for the Boy Scouts of America."

—Don Wildmon
American Family Association

The cultural warriors of the left have never liked the Boy Scouts and have toiled unceasingly through the media, in the courts, and by pressuring government at all levels to force them to abandon the very values they have instilled in generations of young Americans.

Texas Governor Rick Perry knows the value of Scouting. The values that led him to a life of public service and eventually the governorship of his beloved Texas were instilled in him as he worked to become an Eagle Scout in his youth and he acknowledges the debt in this examination of Scouting's value and the almost incomprehensible savagery of the left's assault on a treasured institution.

—David Keene
President, American Conservative Union

On My Honor, a new book by Texas Governor Rick Perry, provides insight on how the American left has waged war on Middle America for over 30 years. By detailing the attacks on the Boy Scouts by the ACLU and others in the secular front, Perry brings to life the broader culture war and the sustainability of the basic scouting values in withstanding the onslaught from the left. This is a book that every American Family concerned about the decline of our culture should read.

—Ken Blackwell
Former Ohio Treasurer, and current Senior Fellow
at both the Family Research Council and the Buckeye Institute

For decades, the culture warriors of the left have waged war on societal institutions that espouse traditional American values. In *On My Honor*, Texas Governor Rick Perry examines the left's attacks on a venerable American institution that has had a profound impact on the values and virtues of young Americans: the Boy Scouts of America.

Demonstrating that no one is immune from their effort to make society conform to their narrow, secular agenda aimed at elevating the individual to a place worthy only of God, the American Civil Liberties Union and their sympathetic counter-culture warriors have waged a legal war of attrition against the Scouts, draining their limited resources with numerous lawsuits and appeals. Their calculated campaign against an institution that teaches young men how to be good stewards of the environment, to respond to emergencies, to be resourceful and thrifty, and to be reverent to adults and God, is chronicled in this thought-provoking book. Perry pulls no punches. He also makes the case for why Scouting is more important than ever in combating the nihilistic forces of our culture and shaping young lives into service-oriented leaders. This book needed to be written, and more importantly, needs to be read by any American Family interested in reclaiming our culture.

—Newt Gingrich

Dedication

To my son Griffin, who persevered in the pursuit of his Eagle in the midst of many distractions common to a young man; my daughter Sydney, who inspires me to appeal to the better angels inside us all; and to my wife Anita, who is eternally patient with all my hobbies but especially supportive of all the time I have dedicated to a more vibrant Scouting movement.

All author profits from this book are dedicated to the Boy Scouts of America, Legal Defense. They continue to be under attack from the forces of secularism, and they can use every bit of financial assistance available from a sympathetic public.

Contents

Foreword

Think what a greater country we would have if everyone lived the principles of Scouting every day. We would all

be *prepared* . . .
do our best *to do our duty to God and Country,*
help other people at all times;
and *keep ourselves physically strong, mentally awake and morally straight.*

Scouting teaches leadership, and our country must have a steady supply of strong leaders to assure that we will continue to grow and improve.

As you read this book, remember that the last phrase of "The Star Spangled Banner" is a question: "Oh, say, does that star-spangled banner yet wave / O'er the land of the free and the home of the brave?"

If all of us were to live the principles of Scouting, the answer would always be a resounding *yes*!

I commend Governor Rick Perry for making time in his busy schedule to write this book and to spell out the danger to Scouting that is posed by people and groups who want to change its guiding principles to suit their slanted views.

My hope is that this book will inspire hundreds, thousands—even millions—of young men to live the principles of Scouting!

—Ross Perot

Acknowledgments

My thanks go to several men who were my companions in Scouting or good Scouting comrades as adults. They are Dr. Russell Dressen; Dr. Mike Overton and Waller Overton, sons of Gene Overton, my scoutmaster; Riley Couch and Bill Andrews. They gave generously of their time to share memories of our Scouting days together and gave their views of the efforts of the ACLU and others to force Scouting to change its values.

I asked several men of accomplishment in their fields for their thoughts on Scouting and where it is heading. All were Eagle Scouts, including: United States Senator Thad Cochran; U.S. Secretary of Defense Robert Gates; Dr. Gordon Gee, now president of Ohio State University and recent chancellor of Vanderbilt University; Astronaut James Lovell; and former FBI Director William Sessions. They made time for me to interview them, and I greatly appreciate their willingness to do so.

Teresa Hartnett, my literary agent, gave valuable advice about the organization of the book and arranged for its publication. My editors at Stroud & Hall made many good suggestions.

Several senior staff members at the Boy Scouts of America provided historical and organizational information, including David Parks, General Council; Connie Adams, Manager, Records Management; George Trosko, Director of the Boy Scout Division; and Stephen Mendlicott, Director of the Marketing & Communications Division.

George Davidson of Hughes Hubbard & Reed, LLP, the BSA's outside legal counsel, was helpful in supplying information about the lawsuits in which the Boy Scouts of America has been involved in its fight to maintain its values and criteria. Mindy Schmutter, a paralegal at the firm, was also helpful.

My former communications director and speechwriter of eight years, Eric Bearse, made numerous edits and suggestions to the manuscript. He has a special gift for putting my most deeply held beliefs into writing. For that I am grateful.

My political consultant, an avid Eagle Scout himself, David Carney, made numerous suggestions for this book and played an invaluable role in keeping the project on target. His ideas were essential.

Robert Hardwicke, a veteran adult Scout leader in California, supplied a useful "grassroots" perspective on current-day Scouting procedures and practices. The research work of Martin Wooster and the many hours of editing by Peter Hannaford are also appreciated.

And finally, with great love and admiration, I would like to acknowledge Gene Overton, my late scoutmaster in Paint Creek, Texas, who inspired and guided me as so many other scout leaders have done for almost a century.

Introduction

You may be wondering, "Why would the governor of the second largest state choose to write his very first book about the Boy Scouts?" Or you may be thinking, "Why should I care what the governor of the second largest state has to say about the Scouts? And who is the governor of the second largest state, anyway?" If your question is the last one, don't worry; you fit into the same category as the vast majority of Americans. If, however, you asked one of the first two questions, I can assure you this book is for you.

Though these pages contain plenty of my personal thoughts, this book is not about me. To the extent that it is about me it is merely a reflection of the fact that I can't view Scouting from any other perspective than my own. I have fifty years of observations packed inside these pages, but whether you like me more or less after reading them isn't really what matters. What does matter is whether, after reading this book, you have a more profound appreciation for the impact Scouting has on both young men and women, and what it means to the preservation of a core decency that has defined American society for 200 years. As you will read, I believe that core decency is at risk if our society continues to drift from the virtues of liberty to the vices of license.

I also believe this book demonstrates that the so-called "War on the Scouts" is a microcosm of a larger phenomenon, a "culture war" that has been tearing at the seams of our society for forty years, and that pits traditional values such as service, selflessness. and sacrifice for the common good against a newer doctrine that elevates the self above society and relegates morality to a shapeless form of relativity. The attacks on the Scouts are but one front in a larger war. The forces of moral relativity—the most famous of which is the American Civil Liberties Union (ACLU)—would remove any mention of God from the public square, would sanitize our society of bright lines dividing right and wrong, and would elevate doing what "feels good" as a moral imperative higher than doing what is necessary for us to live together.

I am passionate about this subject because Scouting was central to my life as a young boy growing up on the rolling plains of West Texas.

And it has remained so. I went to Texas A&M, in part, because I held in awe my Aggie scoutmaster, Gene Overton. He took me as a young boy on my first visit to the campus. I knew from that day onward where I wanted to attend college. As an adult and as an assistant scoutmaster, I passed along Scouting's great traditions to my son. I have never been prouder than I was the day he earned Scouting's highest honor, the Eagle Award. As governor of Texas, I have attended numerous Scouting dinners to raise money for local troops and councils, knowing that Scouting's impact on those young men had the potential to overcome the very different lessons taught by a deteriorating culture.

Once an unassailable American institution, Scouting began coming under attack in 1976. An Oregon girl who had been denied membership in a Cub Scout pack sued the Boy Scouts of America for admission. Most Americans probably didn't think much of that suit at the time because, like me, most didn't even know about it. I was flying a C-130 on tactical airlifts to South America, Europe, and the Middle East as a pilot in the United States Air Force. As such, I was relearning through international travel what I had been taught as a young Scout: that America is unique because Americans understand that freedom is not the same as license, and that it comes with social obligations. One such obligation is to defend freedom with one's life, as I was willing to do and many before me and after me have done. In my case, that calling never took me to the field of battle. I was fortunate. Many others have faced the horror of war in order to further freedom, and many of those citizen-soldiers were prepared at a young age in the Boy Scouts of America.

I left the Air Force in 1977 and returned to the family farm and ranch, renewing friendships with old Scouting comrades. They began to tell me about other lawsuits against the BSA. Up to the 1990s, most had to do with membership (that is, girls wanting to join Boy Scout troops or Cub packs) or employment.

As the years went on, the number of lawsuits seemed to increase and the nature of the suits began to change. Now it was atheists suing the Scouts on the basis of "discrimination," objecting to the pluralistic faith statement in the Scout Oath: "On my honor I will do my best to do my duty to God."

By then the ACLU was knee-deep in the litigious assault on the Scouts, which, on its face, seemed a little odd and ironic since they are an organization dedicated to free speech. Here they were objecting to another organization expressing its views through the personal beliefs of its members.

Along with suits by atheists, some openly homosexual men who had been denied leadership positions in Scout troops sued the Scouts. Like the atheists, they claimed discrimination.

What was going on? Scouting's values are drawn from those of the huge middle class of our nation—a body of people generous to those less fortunate and not envious of those who do well because opportunities are open to nearly everyone.

Reading up on the lawsuits filed against the Boy Scouts of America and some of its units, I saw a clear pattern. The ACLU and its allies seemed determined to force the Boy Scouts to bend to their version of what is right and wrong, with the effort climaxing in 2000 with the Dale case.

In that case, an openly homosexual man in New Jersey claimed that the Boy Scouts violated his state's anti-discrimination law. The state's supreme court sided with him. The suit went all the way to the United States Supreme Court, which ruled that a state may not prohibit the Boy Scouts from adhering to a moral point of view and expressing it in internal leadership policy. It also held that the New Jersey Supreme Court's decision violated the Boy Scouts' First Amendment right to freedom of association.

Most Americans have a live-and-let-live view about homosexuality. After all, many have relatives or acquaintances who are homosexual. Scouting's leaders have the same tolerant view, but they do not believe that someone whose personal agenda is to make an open issue of his sexual orientation should be a Scout leader. Scouting is not about sex, but about building character.

As for the atheist cases, Scouts, like most Americans, believe in God. Scouting is firmly non-sectarian, but it expects its members to express a belief in the Almighty, and to live according to that faith in their daily lives.

The Dale case seemed to clear the way for the Scouts to go forward with their stated mission, the Scout Law, and the Scout Oath, but the ACLU and its allies had other ideas. They have since changed tactics, stepping up their assault on the Scouts through a series of threats and suits intended to prevent Scout groups from using public facilities for their meetings. Are these acts revenge for the Dale case ruling? Only they know, but isn't it odd that the ACLU, which champions First Amendment rights, wants them applied selectively? It seems some of the most intolerant acts occur in the name of tolerance: a paradox that seems to describe much of the ACLU's political agenda.

As I became involved in public service, and my son ascended through the Scouting ranks, my passion for Scouting and my desire to see this American institution treated fairly led me to study the cases and to talk with Scouting leaders about the larger issues of which the assault on the Boy Scouts was a part.

The Culture War

It's called the culture war today, but when it began in the 1960s and '70s, it didn't have a name. Student campus unrest, rejection of authority, the "self-esteem" movement, moral relativism, and the demands of secularists all gradually fused into a series of attacks on American institutions.

It's not that the public didn't have a right to be "skeptical" about institutions such as government (after all, President Nixon, in the Watergate affairs, damaged public trust in the presidency), but the counterculture movement seemed to move beyond a healthy skepticism to a poisonous form of cynicism. Instead of reforming the institution of government, some advocated simply "tuning out" and turning to the carnage of mind-altering addiction.

Others seemed to have a more sinister motive than mere self-indulgence. The objectives of radicals seemed to be to tear away at the foundations of our society, attacking the role of faith, undermining the role of family, and exploiting freedom to push a divisive agenda of permissiveness. From time to time, the outgrowth of this movement has been captured in the public eye by symbolic attacks on beloved symbols and cherished traditions. Radicals file suits to drive religion from the public square and eliminate references to God from the Pledge of Allegiance, currency, and government buildings. They have used lifetime appointments on the judicial bench to advance by decision that which they can't achieve by legislation. They have created a climate of paranoia in our schools, making teachers and administrators into sensitivity police who feel compelled to scold children for wishing someone a Merry Christmas or bringing a classmate a gift. And, as we shall see in the succeeding chapters, they attacked a century-old American institution, the Boy Scouts of America, to make it fit their narrow view of the world.

In this book you will learn . . .

WHO is behind the attacks on the Boy Scouts;

WHAT they have done and are doing to force the Scouts to bend to their will;

WHERE they have launched their attacks;

HOW they intend to remake Scouting and how the Boy Scouts are fighting back.

Although the first attacks on the Boy Scouts seemed isolated and uncoordinated thirty years ago, we now see them as part of a larger movement to redefine American values. If viewed in isolation, one might be tempted to see these attacks as a small affair with little relevance to the lives of most Americans. If seen, however, in the wider context of a great debate taking place in our society, with the attacks on Scouting being merely symptomatic of the clash about the relevancy of traditional American values, then one is more likely to join the chorus of the once silent majority who are now beginning to speak out about protecting the role of faith and family in our society, and preventing the corrosive impact of the culture on our children.

Scouts, their parents, and their leaders care about the outcome of these assaults on Scouting. Even if you are not one of these, you should care, too. We are close to a tipping point in American society. If you believe there is right and wrong, that there are acceptable standards of behavior, that ethics cannot be made up on the spot, that judges should base their decisions on interpretations of the law not current popular opinion, and that this is a nation founded on a belief in God (George Washington called it "Divine Providence"), then you have a stake in this war.

If the attackers win many more victories—either through intimidation, threatened lawsuits, or rulings from kindred judges—the culture war may be lost before we know it. If that happens, we will find ourselves living in a world where moral relativism reigns and individualism runs amok. Now is the time to enlist in this effort, to stand up and be counted.

My perspective is that of an Eagle Scout who worked years to obtain Scouting's highest recognition and who encouraged his son to pursue the same path. I will tell you how Scouting shaped my life and prepared me for young adult challenges, such as serving in the Corps of Cadets at Texas A&M University, flying C-130 tactical airlift in the United States Air Force, and undertaking a career in elected public service, beginning in 1985.

For this book, I have interviewed a number of former Scouts—including some prominent Eagle Scouts—to probe the impact of Scouting on their lives. I've also related the stories of several boys whose Scouting experience made major positive changes in their lives.

I have reviewed what the opponents of Scouting have been saying, too. Despite their assumption that the Boy Scout movement is static, it is not. It is dynamic, and in these pages I will show you both Scouting's history and the changes it has made over time to remain relevant to each new generation of young people.

In these chapters I have examined in detail the issues that have led to the attacks on Scouting and the forces in American society that have organized and carried out those attacks. I have discussed the tactics of those seeking to drive God from the public square and the irony that those who attack the Scouts in the name of religious freedom will, if successful, actually suppress freedom of religion. The book also explains the Scouts' refusal to bend to the winds of "political correctness" by allowing activist homosexual scoutmasters.

The ramifications of the legal challenges to Scouting are examined, including how the Boy Scouts of America (BSA) has responded and—essentially—prevailed. Examining recent polling data, I have compared Scouting's program and values with broader trends in values in American society. As you will see, Scouting's values fit closely with those of society as a whole.

What of the future? In the final chapter, I discuss the choice facing Scouting and American society as a whole—a choice between retaining a set of values encapsulated by a dedication to service to others (and the institutions that carry those values and service forward) on the one hand, and the forces of nihilism and self-centeredness on the other.

When you have completed reading *On My Honor*, I hope you will agree with me that the American values of the Boy Scouts are definitely worth keeping and fighting for.

The Road from Paint Creek

In some respects, Paint Creek is more an idea than a place; a reaffirmation that there is more to life than the rush of people going to and from work, living their stress-filled lives on their small slices of developed land, hoping that their 1.9 children will one day be prosperous enough to enjoy what they themselves never will. Even a casual listener of the Dave Matthews Band or The Police must nod his/her head in ascent at the notion that we are all like "ants marching" or "packed like lemmings into shiny metal boxes, contestants in a suicidal race." Life should be simpler, slower. We should have more meals with our family, with the television turned off and conversation turned on. We should be freed from work when we leave the office, not tethered to it with a Blackberry, a cell phone, and the voice of the boss ringing through our heads. We should be what we were meant to be, and we long for a place to bring us back to such a simpler time.

To some, Paint Creek is a throw-back in time—a fading memory of the way things used to be, when you knew everyone within a 15-mile radius of you, and when you saw each other at work or school and then later at church. Paint Creek reminds me of a sense of community that seems lost today. Back then, if you lost a family member or the rains flooded your property, everybody would be at your door. For me, Paint Creek was not merely an idea; it was the center of civilization, and everything else was an alternative universe.

Our spot of farmland was perched along the rolling plains of West Texas. Dad called our area the Big Empty. I called it paradise. I had thousands of acres to explore, a dog I called my own, and a Shetland pony. We had every amenity a boy could need: electricity because the Rural Electrification Agency, REA, had made its way out our road; a 14-foot-deep water well in lieu of running water (the distinct taste and sight of which, cloudy with minerals, I can still conjure up today); a 1920s bungalow-style house with six rooms (including the bathroom); a radio to listen to weather reports; a Number Two washtub for taking a bath; and a fresh garden by the side of the house, fresh milk from the cow in the pasture, and free-range eggs from the chicken coop. If we were deprived of anything, no one told me. Life was good.

Paint Creek had a school—in fact, you might say the school *was* Paint Creek, because our community's life revolved around it. Some of the teachers and administrators even lived on school property. It was the result of consolidation in the 1930s of several one-room schools. I was one of 110 kids in grades 1 through 12 (there was no kindergarten then). I was fortunate to graduate in the top ten of my class . . . of thirteen students.

A small school in a small community meant there were no secrets. If I misbehaved in class, mom would find out about it before I got home (and so would everyone else within 10 miles). Like a lot of kids in that day, I knew I would not only have to explain my actions to mom, but to dad when he came back from the field that night. Dad believed in the pain principle. His leather belt was usually the delivery method of choice.

There are no boundaries to Paint Creek because it's not a city. The school district was the closest thing to a local unit of government. We were under the jurisdiction of the county government. We measured distances in large gulps. Our nearest neighbor was several hundred yards away. The next closest was miles away. City life was a full 16 miles away—Haskell, the county seat. And the booming metropolis of Abilene was a full hour south. My dad was a county commissioner for 28 years. His district had 328 voters, spread out over 225 square miles. Everyone knew one another. If your road hadn't been graveled on schedule by the county road crew, you'd catch my dad at church or at that week's six-man football game to bend his ear about it.

Like a lot of small West Texas communities then and now, change was measured in stores or churches closing, not opening. Even to this day, with the rest of Texas growing at almost unsustainable rates, my home county of Haskell is one of the few areas of the state that continues to lose population. The store that sold ice cream and Coca-Cola—across the street from the school—closed while I was a boy. We had a Baptist church and a Methodist church and we were involved in both. Over time, though, Paint Creek couldn't sustain two churches, and now only has one.

Life revolved around school, church, and—for most boys—the Boy Scouts. We were too far out in the country for most other activities. I tried to play baseball one summer, but it was too much of a chore to get me to all the practices and games. I did play school sports, such as basketball and football. Of course, football in a community that size involved six boys per side, with many playing on both sides of the ball. Some old film reminded me recently just how far football offenses have progressed since that time. We ran just about the same play every time, which usually meant me throwing my body at a defender so the fastest guy on the team could get loose in their backfield.

Through the years, the greatest extracurricular constant for most of us boys was Scouting. That wasn't the case in every small community in Texas. In some farming areas 4H and Future Farmers of America were the activities around which young people focused their energy. In cities it may have been Boys' and Girls' Clubs. In Paint Creek it was the Boy Scouts.

Like most kids, when I became a teenager, I was unaware that my adult personality was forming itself around the principles, characteristics, and morals instilled by my parents and other adults I admired, such as my scoutmaster. It wasn't just about learning the right manners—make your bed, brush your teeth, clean your room, and do your chores—it was about the larger life lessons: treat everyone with respect, follow the Golden Rule (do unto others as you would have them do unto you), help others who are less fortunate, set goals and work hard to achieve them, take responsibility for your actions, and tolerate differences in others even if you disagree with them. There was a special one in my family: public service is an honorable calling, even a duty.

That idea had run in the family for a century, beginning with my great-great-grandfather, D. H. Hamilton. After experiencing defeat at the hands of Union General Joshua Chamberlain in the Civil War battle at Gettysburg, he returned home to his native East Texas. Hardened from his role as a soldier in the First Texas Infantry, he was no longer the young man his mother had watched march off to war.

He made a life in East Texas, even representing his territory in the Texas House for two years in the 1890s, before family economics drove him westward. He settled around Paint Creek. The local Indians gave it that name for the red color of its clay banks. Paint Creek has been the home of the Perry family since great-great-grandfather Hamilton struck out for a better way of life (though right now it is only my mom and dad living out in Haskell County after our move to Austin in 1991, which was required by state law when I was elected to statewide office).

One of the reasons I looked forward to Saturday, beyond the fact that it provided a reprieve from school, was because I would join my buddies for a Scouting adventure that often lasted all day. On any given Saturday, our parents (or one of our buddies with a "hardship" license for driving farm vehicles) would drive us to our 9 a.m. troop meeting. Once every three months we would even venture off for the weekend, often to Camp Tonkawa just outside Buffalo Gap State Park. The Scouts leased the camp from the state park system in exchange for maintaining it. It was heaven. Camping out, exploring nature, finding wildlife, learning new skills, hearing old war stories: it beat chores at home or, for that matter, hanging out with my older sister, Milla, and her friends.

There, Troop 48 scoutmaster Gene Overton would lead us. He was a 1931 graduate of Texas A&M College, and, like most Aggies of that generation, a veteran of World War II. He turned me on to Texas A&M at a young age. Even though no prior generation of my immediate family had gone to college, for me it was a no-brainer because of how Gene Overton talked about his days in College Station.

I also grew up in a home with a World War II veteran: My dad went off to war when he was eighteen, serving as a tailgunner on a B-17 bomber that flew dozens of missions over Europe. When he returned home, he wasn't thinking about college, but simply settling down and working the farm in his quiet corner of the world, just glad to see the world at peace. Though Paint Creek remained the center of my life, by the age of eighteen I had developed a sense that there was more to life than what it offered. By going to Texas A&M, I knew I could not only fulfill the yearning for something new, but, as an Aggie cadet, I could follow in the military footsteps of my father and Mr. Overton.

The importance of service was a continual theme with Mr. Overton. All the stories he told about A&M, or the Third Army in World War II, had to do with people who had, or one day would, lay their lives on the line. Even today every Aggie Cadet is reminded that during World War II Texas A&M sent more officers into battle than all the military academies combined. Military service is part of the Aggie DNA.

But we boys of Troop 48 didn't just hear about service from Mr. Overton; he modeled it. He was the superintendent of our Sunday school and president of the school board. No man did I respect more as a young kid, with the exception of my father. Mr. Overton could have descended from Mount Sinai. What he said was the law.

We had Camporees a number of times a year at various places. Mr. Overton often arranged for them to be held on ranches owned by his Texas A&M friends. About the time I finished the requirements for Eagle Scout, and I had just reached my fourteenth birthday, we went to the National Jamboree at Valley Forge, Pennsylvania. I recall President Lyndon Johnson landing there in a helicopter, as well as Lady Baden-Powell (the widow of Scouting's founder) from England. For a fourteen-year-old I had what seemed the adventure of a lifetime with my Scouting travels: the 1964 World's Fair in New York City, the Liberty Bell in Philadelphia, meeting government leaders in Washington, D.C., and camping at Valley Forge.

Until then, I'd never been outside of Texas except for a summer vacation in a log cabin at Estes Park, Colorado. It was such a seminal event in my life that I still have the diary I kept on the trip as the troop scribe, with entries about the historic sites of Washington, a wound I acquired on the trip, and how attractive the stewardesses were on my maiden commercial flight. In 1964 I not only attended the National Jamboree, but I was also elected to the Order of the Arrow. It's not a secret society, but rather the Brotherhood of Honor campers, selected by the Scouts themselves to go to the next level of learning and service.

Growing up in Paint Creek, I thought the things we were taught as Scouts—to do our best to be trustworthy, loyal, helpful, friendly, courteous, kind, obedient, cheerful, thrifty, brave, clean, and reverent—were pretty much what the Founding Fathers had intended for succeeding generations when they created our nation.

When I got to Texas A&M I was not confronted by the student unrest that was gripping campuses in the late 1960s; A&M remained a conservative place dedicated to training military officers. Still, my friends and I certainly heard a lot about turmoil. Opposition to authority of any kind was taking hold on many campuses. Those who spoke against the counterculture activists were shouted off many a campus stage. This didn't square with what I'd learned in Scouting. What had happened to decency and tolerance? What happened to civil disagreement and social responsibility? The clamor for drugs and disdain for the institutions that had guided our nation successfully for nearly 200 years seemed to be sweeping the country. Some seemed to want to knock the world as we knew it off its hinges, without replacing it with anything of value.

When I graduated, our nation was still embroiled in Vietnam. I received my commission in the Air Force, earned my pilot's wings, and jumped into the co-pilot seat of a C-130. Not fancy flying, like the jet fighters, but nonetheless significant for moving soldiers and munitions to critical theaters of operation.

Coming from a small community like Paint Creek, and a somewhat insular culture at Texas A&M, I found being thrust into the role of international traveler courtesy of Uncle Sam to be an eye-opening experience. I saw the beaches of Rio De Janiero, the old cities of Europe that existed long before Columbus ever set sail for the Americas, and the sands of the Persian Gulf, occupied by Bedouins who seemed stuck in a previous century. One time, driving in a military vehicle on a desert stretch of road in the Arabian Peninsula, I saw a pickup trucking heading toward us and thought for a second I was in Paint Creek with the family dog poking his head around the corner of the cab to catch some fresh air. When we got a little closer, I noticed it was a camel in the bed of the pickup, his tongue flapping in the wind and his legs folded. I knew then I was a long way from home.

The fun that ensued from our travels was balanced by a growing sensation of homesickness. I learned that, despite the upheaval on the home front and the economic turmoil experienced in the '70s, America remained unique in the world, a place where a sense of opportunity pervaded, even for kids raised on tenant farms and children born in one-room shacks. The sense of class division that so permeates foreign societies—including those of affluent, freedom-loving allies such Britain—is not a barrier in American society. Sure, there are exclusive clubs and moneyed schools whose supporters take care of their own. The middle-class kid, however, is not shut off from pursuing a dream or a profit. In places such as Saudi Arabia, if you weren't born into the right family, your fate was already more or less decided. I have found that when people can't dream, hopelessness gives way to despair, and despair can express itself in extremism and violence.

After four and a half years in the Air Force, I yearned for new opportunities at home. In 1977 I left the service as a captain to return to Texas to help my mom and dad on the farm. That was a difficult year to say the least—returning as a grown man to the place I had only known as a boy. Dad still thought I was there to do chores. I reminded him that I had just finished commanding a multimillion-dollar piece of government equipment and a number of grown men. He reminded me that the chores still needed tending to. You could say there was a transitional period where dad and I didn't always see eye to eye. Because of that, and because we went through one of our famous droughts, I began interviewing for a job as a commercial pilot. Yet, as if God was talking to me directly, he opened the heavens with a storm that deluged the rolling plains of the Big Empty. I got the apparent message: I would stick with farming for a spell longer.

Dad and I subsequently worked together for a number of years, and steadily became partners and best friends instead of just father and son. During the same time period I also wore down my high school sweetheart, Anita Thigpen, and convinced her to be my wife, for better or for worse. Thus, the wandering twenty-seven-year-old who came home from the Air Force felt a little settled—for a while. Because besides working the land, what the Perrys do is run for elected office.

After settling in Haskell County, my great-great-grandfather was elected county judge from 1900–1904. My great-grandfather was elected a county commissioner. After him, my grandfather, Hoyt Perry, ran for county commissioner in the 1940s, but was defeated. My father, Ray, lost the first time he ran for county commissioner in 1964, but he was elected in 1968 and served for seven consecutive terms until retiring in 1996.

The urge to get involved in public service was strong for me. It wasn't as if I aspired to be governor from the age of seven, but I knew growing up—because of my family tradition and because of the values I learned in Scouting—that giving back in the form of public service was an important principle.

Just as the weather had kept me from leaving the family vocation, it almost prevented me from seizing an opportunity to pursue the other family tradition of public service. This time, in late December, an ice storm shut down our part of the country. The power went out. News slowed to a crawl. The roads were icy—a phenomenon made worse by the fact that Texans were the ones driving on them.

After going stir-crazy for a few days, I finally got up the courage to go into town. I saw an old friend at a café who asked me if I was running for Representative Hanna's seat. I told him there was no way in hell I would take on the incumbent in the primary. He said Mr. Hanna had announced in Austin a few weeks ago that he was retiring. My heart felt as if it had stopped. I had no indication this opportunity would become available, and I had no idea how to proceed. A decision had to be made quickly, for the filing deadline was days away.

Anita and I hadn't been married even two years, and I was getting ready to propose I spend a lot of time away from her and our newborn son Griffin. We didn't have the luxury of a drawn-out discussion over weeks and months. It was time either to jump in impulsively, or pass. One factor: I was getting restless with life on the farm. Anita saw how much I wanted to do this. After all, she knew what Perrys did: they ran for office.

Thus, in 1984, I was elected to the Texas legislature representing Haskell County and seven other rural counties in my part of the state. I served on the House Appropriations, Energy, and agenda-setting Calendar committees during my three terms.

In 1989, I switched political parties—a traumatic event for someone who was raised in a "yellow dog" Democrat family (the idea being that one would vote for a yellow dog before voting for a Republican). Soon after, I took an even bigger gamble: announcing I would run for statewide office against incumbent Democrat and national populist figure Jim Hightower.

No one said I had a chance. The voters said something different, electing me in a squeaker as state commissioner of agriculture in 1990. Then, in 1998, I won a close contest for lieutenant governor against my old Aggie classmate (and fellow Squadron 6 Flying Tiger) John Sharp. When Governor George W. Bush was elected president, I became governor. I was elected to a full term in 2002 and reelected in 2006.

I can't say that Scouting planted the idea of public service in my head, but I can say it prepared me for it. It prepared me to run focused, disciplined campaigns where I didn't worry about what my opponent was saying about me, but instead focused on the job of being a candidate. On those long days on the fundraising circuit, when I was tired of shaking hands, tired of rubber chicken, and ready to scream at my staff, I would go back to the Scouting admonition to be kind. Perseverance got me through late-night hearings in the capitol . . . another trait learned in the Scouts. At some point, just about every trait advocated by Scouting came to bear during tough campaigns and heated negotiations, and they kept me from making costly mistakes.

If Scouting can lead me down the right path, I believe it can continue to do the same for young men and young women across America regardless of their circumstances. We need people of all backgrounds and ways of life to answer the call of service—to echo the words of the Prophet Isaiah in a more secular sense of the expression: "Here am I, send me."

Public service isn't drudgery reserved for someone else, but the high calling placed upon my life. I hope more and more young men will answer that calling because of their time in the Scouts.

Two Sides of a Coin: Scouting and Public Service

Scouting, despite lawsuits and maneuverings against its use of public facilities for meetings and events, is in strong shape. There are more than four million active Scouts and adult volunteers today. Public service, on the other hand, has fallen on hard times.

In recent times, two members of Congress have gone to prison for bribery. Another has been indicted. Others are under investigation. Prominent public officials confess to extramarital affairs and acts of public lewdness. Congress's approval rating, as I write this in summer 2007, stands at 14 percent. No wonder many qualified men and women say "thanks, but no thanks" to their parties' candidate recruitment committees.

There is no one reason for this. Some say the appeal of public service—either temporarily or as a career—began to decline after the counterculture upheavals of the late sixties, followed by Watergate. Certainly the so-called "mainstream media" seemed to increase their skepticism and cynicism about the actions and motives of public officials after that time. Also, the advent of 24-hour-a-day news channels intensified the coverage of allegations, investigations, indictments, and court cases involving public officials.

The doings of disgraced lobbyist Jack Abramoff shed a sharper-than-ever light on the role that greed can play in Washington. Those who took money for their votes betrayed their calling to public service. Those who simply took free golfing trips without disclosing them had forgotten that public service requires something of a Caesar's-wife approach to the acceptance of favors while in office.

When a boy becomes a Scout, he takes an oath—a promise—that "On my honor I will do my best to do my duty to God and my country and to obey the Scout Law; to help other people at all times; to keep myself physically strong, mentally awake, and morally straight."

The Scout Law that he pledges to obey says, "A Scout is trustworthy, loyal, helpful, friendly, courteous, kind, obedient, cheerful, thrifty, brave, clean, and reverent."

The Scout motto he adopts is "Be prepared."

And the Scout slogan is "Do a good turn daily."

Nobody is perfect, of course, but all of this is a recipe for good behavior and good citizenship and can open one's thoughts to serving others in a public capacity.

For me, public service was a family tradition. When I became a Scout, the Scout Oath and Law reinforced the principles that came out of that tradition.

Public service of one kind or another seems to come naturally to many who have been active in Scouting. Recently, I saw a list of famous men in public life who had been Eagle Scouts. I decided to interview several of them to get their views on public service and its relationship to Scouting. Those I interviewed are U.S. Senator Thad Cochran, who experienced Scouting in his native Mississippi; U.S. Secretary of Defense Robert S. Gates, whose Scouting career was in his native Kansas; Dr. E. Gordon Gee, president of Ohio State University, who did his Scouting in his native state, Utah; former astronaut, Navy Captain (Ret.) James A. Lovell, who was born in Cleveland but did his Scouting in Indiana; and William Sessions, former director of the Federal Bureau of Investigation and former chief judge of the Federal District Court of West Texas, who began his Scouting in Nebraska and completed it in Kansas City, Missouri.

In all the interviews, I found that each man felt that his Scout training contributed to his later successes. For example, I asked, "Were there any particular elements of your Scouting experience that proved helpful along the way?" The examples varied, but the impact of Scouting on each man was strong:

• "Learning that you really have to earn advancement in life just as you really have to earn merit badges was a major lesson. I learned it when I flunked my first try for the Civics merit badge." —Senator Cochran
• "At age fourteen I attended what was then known as the National Junior Leadership Training Course at Philmont Scout Ranch in New Mexico. I have always felt that those two weeks taught me the basics of leadership and management." —Secretary Gates
• "Scouting had an impact on my ability to engage in academic life. It provided intellectual stimulation, discipline, and the ability to work under pressure." —Dr. Gee
• "Through Scouting I was exposed to astronomy and science. With fellow Scouts I built rockets. [As a result,] I wanted to become a rocket engineer." —Captain Lovell
• "The Scout Oath and Scout Law were fundamental for me. The experience of staying focused on important matters must have come, in part, from doing the work that had to be done to achieve the Eagle badge." —Judge Sessions

Despite the variety in their public service careers, all five men answered the next question in ways that struck a common theme: "What one word best describes the role and value of Scouting in today's world?"

• "It's three words, but 'nurturing leadership possibilities' in the youth of our great great country sums it up for me." —Senator Cochran
• "Character-building." —Secretary Gates
• "I think it is 'values.'" —Dr. Gee
• "My vote goes to the word 'Citizenship.'" —Captain Lovell
• "Character." —Judge Sessions

These men came from different places and different backgrounds, but they shared many of the experiences all Boy Scouts share, then worked their way through the rigors of becoming Eagle Scouts. Some 50,000 Boy Scouts are now working on the final stages to make Eagle rank. The experiences of these successful men can be an inspiration to them, but they also show, once again, the positive impact that Scouting can have on the men Boy Scouts are to become. And these successful public servants can also be an inspiration for today's Boy Scouts to consider careers in public service.

Former presidential candidate, and governor of Massachesetts, Michael Dukakis, told me the same thing. He said, "In earning some of those merit badges, I was introduced to the political and civic life of my community at an early age. I'd like to think that that was one of the reasons I chose to pursue a career in public service, and the more young people we can encourage to get involved in the political life of their communities and state and country, the better. Scouting can play an important role in doing just that.

I do not believe the idea of service is passé in America today, but I do believe many prefer to stay in the private sector when they see so much negative attention placed on public servants. Some of that negative attention is the fault of public officials. Some have acted in stupid, sometimes criminal, ways. When good people are scared off, however, the void is often filled by more individuals with questionable character who see service as a means to enrichment and empowerment.

On the way to reaching the top of their respective fields, the men I interviewed faced challenges and overcame them. They believe the principles they learned in Scouting helped them get there. I can say that's doubly true for those who, like me, seek to perform public service through elective office.

Shakespeare had Hamlet ponder whether it was better to "suffer the slings and arrows of outrageous fortune, or take arms against a sea of troubles." Some days, in elective office, it seems as if a sea of troubles surrounds me. I soon learned that the job requires a lot of patience, and once the "sea" calms, I need to make decisions with careful deliberation in order to be as fair as possible to everyone concerned with an issue.

Even then, there are plenty of "slings and arrows" to be deflected. Someone starts a rumor. It moves with the speed of a brush fire on a hot day. By the time you've put it to rest, you have spent a lot of energy and may have had your reputation dented in the process. Sometimes political adversaries put forth wild allegations. Sometimes a journalist with a hidden agenda twists what you have said or an action you have taken in order to suit that agenda.

It's not just a matter of "if you have nothing to hide, you have nothing to worry about." It's not that easy. Sometimes adversaries create smoke where there is no fire. Whenever things seem to be getting rough, I find elements of the Scout Oath and Scout Law to carry me through, such as "On my honor I will do my best to do my duty to God and my country" and the admonition to be courteous and cheerful. And, of course, the Scout motto: "Be prepared."

Lunch with Some Old Scouts

For nearly 100 years Scouting has worked for millions of young American boys of all races and religions, teaching self-discipline, self-reliance, and teamwork. Girl Scouts USA has had a similar impact on young girls across our great country. Yet, the Boy Scouts as an institution has been dragged into a war not of its making—the culture war for America's soul. Scouting's opponents want to make fundamental changes to this successful institution to suit their own view of the world.

If Scouting is to be engaged in such a conflict, I figure it could use a few able-bodied, enthusiastic allies to fight back. That's why I've written this book. In the process of thinking about how I would organize it, I called several companions from my Paint Creek days and others from my involvement in Scouting over the years. I asked them to meet me one day in June 2007 for lunch so we could talk about what Scouting has meant to us and what the future holds for a movement that is dear to us.

There were six of us: Russell Dressen, an optometrist from Abilene, Texas; Waller Overton, eldest son of my scoutmaster and current scoutmaster for Troop 148; Mike Overton, youngest brother to Waller and an Allen, Texas, veterinarian; Bill Andrews, a Ruth's Chris Steak House owner in Austin, Texas; and Riley Couch, a lifelong banker who is closest in age to me (the others are several years older, and a couple were young Scout leaders of my troop).

Sitting around the table, we told stories and talked about what makes Scouting so appealing to us even today, some forty to fifty years since we wore the uniform. It wasn't a theoretical discussion involving Harvard intellectuals; it was the musings of men who grew up in the countryside (some of whom still labor on the land) and who care deeply about the preservation of American values. As Waller Overton put it, "I'm not a philosopher. I love Scouting. I love the program. I love what it does. I love how it can take a young man and put him on the right track and give him some basics to live life by—some rules."

Pretty simple words. Nothing flowery or profound, and yet they express what Scouting is about: our hope that young boys who may or may not have the best guidance at home will take a positive path because of the virtues instilled during the many days they wore the Scout uniform.

To grow into successful adulthood, young people need a support network. When you consider that not every child is born into the best of circumstances, the greatest hope we have is that society's institutions such as the education system, athletic organizations, faith-based communities, or mentoring groups will somehow get to those children in a way their parents do not.

The ideal remains a situation in which a mother and a father spend time with their children, teaching them a sense of social responsibility and self-worth tied to selfless service. This doesn't always happen. Some children fall through the gaps. They have no control over the world they are born into or over the values of their parents. For them, there is a need for civic-minded organizations that develop in them a sense of self-worth that they cannot get from home. Nevertheless, I don't believe a variety of social groups should be able to override the authority of parents.

The great thing about Scouting is that it doesn't manufacture self-worth like the liberal self-esteem movement does. That movement makes "feeling good" a paramount value, supplanting the need to teach children right and wrong for the "greater good" of making them feel good about themselves. Scouting builds self-esteem based on achievement.

As my friend Riley Couch said over lunch, the first thing he thinks about when it comes to Scouting and weekends at Camp Tonkawa are accomplishments: "We completed things, and we received merit badges that proved it. We were recognized. I couldn't have been more proud when I got that Lifesaving merit badge. Very few guys passed that badge at camp. Usually, they had to go back and take it again. After passing it, I thought I had accomplished everything in life I wanted at that point."

Harvard professor Edward O. Wilson put it to me this way:

I grew up in parts of Alabama and northern Florida that offered relatively poor public-school education. The Boy Scouts of America filled much of the gap by offering a superb technique that could well be copied by public schools and colleges everywhere: *self-paced instruction* measured by advancement in rank and in real accomplishment through each of the merit badges offered, all with the help of a scout leader and local mentors. As a boy I was a loner. The BSA, more than the Baptist Church or public schools, socialized me. I learned to work with others. I also absorbed the ethical precepts that form the backbone of Scouting. The Boy Scouts are among the most valuable institutions in this country.

J. W. Marriott, Jr., chairman and CEO of one of the largest hotel chains in the world, shared with me a delightful story about the Scouting merit system:

As I passed First Class rank and started on the road to earning merit badges for my Eagle, I almost gave up over the difficult tasks for the required Camping merit badge. How was a city boy ever going to sleep out-of-doors for fifty days and nights to pass this particular requirement when there was no Scout camp available?

The other camping requirement I had difficulty with was starting a fire with two sticks. One stick was a board with a small hole. This board was placed on the ground and the other stick fit into the hole and was held perpendicular to the board. The idea was to rapidly turn the top stick so the friction in the hole on the board would form a spark that could be placed into tinder shavings. If you blew on the spark it would ignite the shavings and the fire would start.

When I finally appeared before the Camping merit badge counselor, he asked me to use the stick and board to start a fire. Well, I twisted the stick but it only got warm. So I twisted it harder and harder, and faster and faster. It began to smoke, but there was no spark. It smoked some more. I began to breathe hard and fast as I worked. I inhaled the smoke and my eyes began to water. I began to cough and tears were streaming down my face. I was just about ready to quit when, through the smoke, I spotted a small spark which began to show a bright red. It was truly the most beautiful thing I had ever seen! I quickly pushed it into the tinder and began blowing on it until, with what seemed like my last breath, the tinder began to burn. Hallelujah! I had passed the Camping merit badge—my last one before becoming an Eagle.

The Boy Scouts didn't hand out badges for trying. They handed out badges for getting the job done. As opposed to sports leagues today where no one keeps score, the scouts keep score. They taught us that success is measured, not handed to us as an inheritance. They also taught us that life isn't always fair, which was good, because I have since learned that, indeed, life isn't always fair. Artificially prescribed outcomes that ignore effort produce effortless children who don't care much about results; they come to expect that someone will simply manipulate the outcome for them.

Waller Overton candidly confessed that as a scoutmaster today, he often feels like he runs a weekend babysitter service. There is a sad realization that some kids are not enrolled in Scouts to have their lives shaped, but to give their parents a break. God knows, some parents need a break. Can Scouting penetrate through the current pop culture's bombardment of messages to today's child, when its aim is not to entertain that child (as a video game would), but to develop his mind and character through a program of work?

None of my friends sitting around that lunch table were ready to throw in the towel when it came to Scouting's ability to shape young lives in the modern world, but they also seemed to realize the limited reach such an organization can have in a society where there is a dissipated sense of community; a level of detachment where people can live for years next door to others without knowing anything about them—even their names.

My friend Russell Dressen, who was a young adult Scout leader with my troop, expressed a sense of optimism for the future, contingent on a reconnection with the values of our youth. He said, "I think if we maintain the same values we had back in [the] late '50s and early '60s and teach them today to more and more youth, not only does Scouting survive but it also contributes to a stronger country. Scouting is being assailed by various forces, most of which disagree with many of the premises on which Scouting is built. This is a free country, and they are entitled to their own opinions and values. So am I, and I find Scouting's values essential parts of good citizenship."

Is that merely a sentimental view of the past? Certainly that generation had its problems, not the least of which was a soul-searching consternation with the issue of race. I think what Russell speaks of, however, is less a return to a romanticized era and more a return to a strong sense of community, where neighbors invested in the lives of neighbors, and a sense of social responsibility that overwhelmed any instinct to live a life of seclusion. We know our lives are enriched when we live in community, solving one another's problems and bearing one another's burdens.

If my dad found out that I was paddled at school, his first question of the principal would be, "What did the boy do wrong?" It wasn't ever a question about whether someone who didn't share my bloodline had the right to discipline me. It was merely assumed, in a community where parents shared the same interest of raising children to respect authority and live by established values, that other adults exercised their authority in a manner consistent with what was best for the child. If an educator did that today, the threat of a lawsuit wouldn't be far behind. The ability of the community to set guidelines and enforce them is greatly impaired by a litigious climate that has arisen out of distrust among adults who share no sense of community with one another.

You can hear a parent confronting an educator or a Scout leader or a youth pastor, with the question, "What right do you have to discipline my child?" In a society where there are frequent stories about child abuse involving clergy, teachers, and other leaders to whom we entrust our children, I am not without sympathy for the parent who asks such a question. Often, however, the question is really a denial of the bad traits we as parents have allowed in our children. Instead of blaming ourselves for failing our children, we point the finger at someone else. This often comes from an unwillingness to set firm rules and enforce guidelines for our children who, I believe, are crying out for established boundaries. Deep inside, most children do not rebel against authority; they desire it because it shows them they are loved.

A society that puts the rights of individuals above their responsibilities is in danger of creating a generation of children too self-absorbed to contribute to the fabric of community. Scouting resists this temptation—a temptation I believe is as old as original sin in the Garden of Eden, when man began the quest to become his own god instead of settling for the joy and security of submitting to God and living in communion with Him and His creation.

Ask just about any parent, and he or she will tell you that, without proper socialization, our children would gravitate toward their own nature, which is to be selfish without regard for anyone else. They would hit their younger siblings every time to get the toys they want. They would throw a temper tantrum every time to get their way. They would likely eat ice cream instead of broccoli if they got to pick their next meal. In other words, children would not naturally do what is best for them unless adult authorities intervened and used children's natural desire to please to the adults' advantage.

Scouting teaches the value of deferred gratification—that true pride comes from persevering toward a goal. It teaches young men that there are no free rides on the road to success, and that those who reach the top do so because of hard work, determination, and vision.

Scouting also teaches the practical things in life, like how to build a fire, how to tie a knot, how to clean up after camping, how to tend for nature and parklands, how to swim, and how to shoot. One of the most poignant things I recall learning was how to respect, honor, and even retire an American flag. One of the ways of retiring it was to burn it. That meant burning it in an appropriate way that was prescribed by the manual. As I shared with my old Scouting buddies over lunch, I made the mistake of burning a nylon flag. Behind the Scout hut was a one-car garage with a room in the back. It had a fireplace and a chimney. I built a fire in it, did everything as prescribed, and put that flag in the fire. It started to smell like a burnt clutch, and worse yet I thought I was breathing in exhaust from a diesel train. I was almost asphyxiated from the burning nylon, coughing my head off. It was hard to be properly solemn in the midst of overpowering nylon fumes.

Scouting taught Gilmore Thornton, an old buddy of mine, something as basic as how to use cooking utensils—something he had never done prior to his first campout. This is someone who went on to serve as an F-111 Aircraft Commander in the U.S. Air Force. Of course, we knew his potential within weeks of meeting him because he built our first Scout hut on Mr. Overton's property.

We also learned first aid and practiced on the scoutmaster's dog, Tramp. As Waller put it, "He could be seen some Saturdays after the first of our first aid demonstrations hobbling back up to the scoutmaster's house with one foot in a sling and a Band Aid around his head. Tramp was a registered Scout in the troop; he even made First Class rank because he could swim. He passed his swimming test and did it all."

Waller also reminded us of the time Tramp stood trial before the troop: "The boys were cooking one time, and there was some meat setting there ready to cook, and when they turned around it was gone. The cook accused Tramp of eating the meat. Another boy said, 'No, Tramp would not touch that meat.' So they had a trial. They picked a judge, they had a defense attorney and a trial attorney, and they presented the case. The rest of the troop was the jury. The jury decided that Tramp was not guilty; that he could not have taken that meat. It had to have disappeared, evaporated, or been cooked—or something. So he was let off."

A trust develops between Scouts that goes with them the rest of their lives. My friend Bill Andrews, who owns the Ruth's Chris Steak House franchise in Austin, reflected during our lunch on the difficulty of finding good employees: "Trustworthiness is a trait that is sometimes hard to find. People want jobs, but they don't want to work. People want you to pay them, but they don't necessarily want to go by your rules or do what is best for the customers. A lot of the traits that I have as a business owner, I learned in Boy Scouts. You treat people the way you want to be treated, give them respect, give them an opportunity, and hope for the best."

If I see "Eagle Scout" on a young man's résumé, I know immediately that he has been tested and has persevered; that he can stick to a task until it is completed; that I can trust him to give his full effort in the advance of our mission. I also know that there's a good chance he persisted in the face of peer pressure. Chances are friends or schoolmates questioned his participation in the Scouts, called him a "do-gooder" or some other moniker to demean his participation, but despite that he saw real value in the lessons he was learning—and plugged away.

The question is, in a world with so many distractions—video games, a variety of children's television programming, iPods, more sporting programs than ever, illegal drugs and alcohol, and so much more—can Scouting still prevail upon the better angels of young men? Or are we beyond the lessons of Scouting in today's society? Can Scouting survive another thirty years like the last thirty, when the forces of the left began systematically to attack its foundations?

Scouting: How It Began, How It Works

A Chance Meeting in the Fog

Before he boarded the train for New York City in August 1909, a friend warned Chicago millionaire publisher William Boyce that the fog in London could be pea-soup thick at that time of year. During the ocean voyage to Southampton, Boyce didn't think much about it, but the fog awaited him when he arrived in London.

The next day he set out on foot for a business appointment, but soon lost his bearings and became lost. The fog was so thick he could see almost nothing beyond a couple of feet. Just then a boy of about twelve appeared out of the gloom, carrying a lantern. The boy asked him if he could be of assistance. "You certainly can," said Boyce. He mentioned the address he was seeking and the boy offered to take him there.

When they arrived at Boyce's destination, he reached in his pocket for a shilling to give the boy. "No thank you, sir," he said. "I am a Scout. I won't take anything for helping."

"What is a Scout?" asked Boyce. The boy told him about the Scouting movement in Britain. Boyce was intrigued. He asked the boy if he would take him to the British Scouting office as soon as his appointment was over. The boy said he would be happy to wait and sat on the steps in the fog.

Later, at the Scout office, Boyce met Lord Robert Baden-Powell, who had earned fame as a general in the battle of Mafeking in 1899 in the Boer War in South Africa. He was especially interested in the techniques of military scouting and wrote a book about it called *Aids to Scouting*. Not long after the book came out, he learned that a number of boys were using his book as a guide to peacetime outdoor activities. That set him to thinking: Why not adapt the concepts of army scouting to a boys' program? Perhaps Baden-Powell's motivation was simply the development of young enthusiasts who would later become army recruits and take up the specialty of scouting—advanced reconnaissance work—in the next war.

In 1904, Baden-Powell met Ernest Thompson Seton at the Savoy Hotel in London. Seton, a Canadian, was a popular and prolific writer about nature and wildlife topics. In 1901–1902, he had created a boys' program called Woodcraft Indians. He gave Baden-Powell a copy of the manual he wrote for the program. Baden-Powell made use of many of Seton's program elements as he put together his own plan, which he "field tested" on a group of boys in 1907. Refining the plan further, he formally organized the Boy Scouts in 1908 and published its first manual. Seton, in the introduction to the Boy Scouts of America's first *Boy Scout Handbook*, made it clear he considered himself the true founder of the Scouting movement. He wrote,

> I went to England to carry on the work [of promoting a "Woodcraft and Scouting movement"] there, and, knowing General R. S. S. Baden-Powell as the chief advocate of Scouting in the British Army, invited him to cooperate with me in making the movement popular. Accordingly, in 1908 he organized his Boy Scout movement, incorporating principles of the [Woodcraft] Indian with other ethical features bearing on savings banks, fire drills, etc., as well as by giving it a partly military organization and a carefully compiled and fascinating book.

Baden-Powell's enthusiasm and description of Scouting and its benefits impressed Boyce. He decided then and there to take Scouting with him to the United States. Once home, Boyce gathered together a group of friends who were business and civic leaders. He briefed them on what he had learned in London. They decided to create an American version of the Boy Scouts. On February 8, 1910, Boyce incorporated the organization in the District of Columbia (to emphasize its intended national scope).

What of the boy whose good turn intrigued William Boyce to learn more and to go on to found a national Scouting movement? The boy never gave his name, but his gesture of aid became the first widely recorded "good turn" that was eventually embodied in the Scout slogan, "Do a good turn daily." Later, American Scouts erected a monument in the shape of an American buffalo at the British Scout Training Center at Gilwell Park in England to honor this unknown Boy Scout.

No Small Dreams: Going National

At the time Boyce was incorporating the Boy Scouts of America, there were several outdoor-oriented groups using the name "Boy Scouts." For example, there were several other independently organized troops based on elements of the British program. To serve as executive secretary of the new BSA, Boyce recruited James West, a Washington, D.C., lawyer, who had worked on many juvenile cases. Boyce arranged for an office to be established and named West as Chief Scout Executive (West expected the job to be temporary; however, he held it from 1911 until 1943 when he retired).

West was an effective organizer. He and Boyce launched a campaign to bring into the BSA the various independent scout groups. Seton merged his Woodcraft Indians into the BSA and served as its first Chief Scout from 1910 to 1915. The only holdout after 1912 was the fiery publisher William Randolph Hearst. He created U.S. Boy Scout three months after the BSA was organized. It was affiliated with the Order of World Scouts, a British program created to compete with Baden-Powell's.

To consolidate its national credentials, the Boy Scouts of America lobbied Congress for legislation that would give it a charter. The enabling legislation was passed in 1916 and signed into law by President Woodrow Wilson.

The charter gave them standing in federal court as they sought to be the nation's sole Scouting organization. Baden-Powell testified in support of the BSA and it ultimately prevailed against U.S. Boy Scouts in 1919, which soon after faded away.

Daniel Carter Beard, a popular magazine illustrator and writer, grew up in Kentucky where the tales of Daniel Boone's exploits inspired him. In 1905 he created The Society of the Sons of Daniel Boone, which became the largest boy's club in the nation. He later renamed it Boy Pioneers of America. When the BSA was incorporated, he was quick to join as one of its leaders, becoming its first National Commissioner and Chairman of the Court of Honor. He designed the Boy Scouts' emblem, a fleur-de-lys with the American eagle and shield. The U.S. Patent Office granted it a design patent in 1911.

As the organization grew, tension between its strong-willed leaders became inevitable. Ernest Thompson Seton saw James West as "just" an administrator, not capable of overseeing the programmatic aspects of Scouting. Seton pushed for a program for younger boys (years later, one was adopted and became the Cub Scouts). West and Beard opposed this. West won the struggle for power, forcing Seton out in 1915 and deleting all of Seton's written contributions to the *Boy Scout Handbook* within a year. Seton then founded the Woodcraft League of America. He later returned to the BSA and in 1926 received its Silver Buffalo award.

They Didn't Forget the Girls

The lives of the Boy Scouts' leaders intertwined in another way: programs for girls. Julia Seton, Ernest's wife, joined with Dan's sister Lina Beard, James West of the BSA, and Luther and Charlotte Vetter Gullick (who are credited as the official founders) to create Camp Fire Girls on March 17, 1910. Today it is named Camp Fire USA. Originally founded for girls, it is now coed, but girls are the main participants.

In 1912 Juliette Gordon "Daisy" Low founded Girl Guides of America, later changing its name to Girl Scouts of America. Today it is named Girl Scouts of the USA. Along with the Boy Scouts of America and the Little League, it is one of only three youth organizations in the nation with a Congressional charter, receiving it in 1950.

In most other countries the girls' equivalent to the Boy Scouts is called Girl Guides (founded in Britain by Robert Baden-Powell's wife, Lady Olave Baden-Powell). In some countries there is no distinction between Boy Scouts and Girl Guides, with both boys and girls participating in coed troops. Other countries offer a single national organization, but with separate troops for Boy Scouts and Girl Guides. In the U.S. the two organizations and their programs are completely separate.

The Girl Scout movement is divided into five divisions: Daisy Girl Scouts (ages 5 and 6), Brownie Girl Scouts (ages 6 to 8), Junior Girl Scouts (ages 8 to 11), and Studio 2B (ages 11 to 17).

The Boy Scout Program at Work

The Boy Scout movement has spread worldwide since Robert Baden-Powell's field test in 1907, with operations in 185 countries. All Scouting organizations are independent from one another, but operate around the general principles developed by Baden-Powell. Some countries, especially in Europe, have separate Scout groups for boys of different religions, languages, or ethnic backgrounds. In the United States, with nearly one million active Boy Scouts, there is a single national organization and program. Within that framework there are programs designed for different age groups and interests. These are the categories:

• Cub Scouts (first through fifth grades);
• Boy Scouts (ages 11 through 17);
• Venturing (originally called Exploring—for young men and women ages 14 through 20).

Scouting's "Big Idea"

As the nineteenth century gave way to the twentieth, and British Army lieutenant-general Robert Baden-Powell mulled the idea of a boys' organization, he may have seen it as a source for recruiting army scouts. He probably reasoned that those who didn't go into the army would benefit from the order and discipline of the program he had in mind.

When Ernest Thompson Seton met Baden-Powell in 1904, they seemed to have an immediate meeting of the minds. Seton's Woodcraft Indian program emphasized nature and wildlife. Many of his ideas became a part of Baden-Powell's first Scouting manual.

Consciously or not, the founders (and later Boyce, West, and Beard) understood that the bodies of boys ages eleven to seventeen undergo rapid changes. These young men are in the process of forming their own personalities, unconsciously drawing traits they admire in their parents, other relatives, teachers, clergy, and other figures in their lives. Often their emotions are unsettled. In fact, I frequently tell Scouts pursuing the Eagle Award to try to achieve it before they get their driver's licenses and before they fall under the spell of "the fumes": car fumes and perfume. I speak from experience.

The founders—and Scouting's leaders ever since—viewed the program as a healthful, wholesome way to channel restless energy; to add structure to the boys' days; and to teach self-reliance, teamwork, leadership skills, and the value of order and organization. The program, with its emphasis on outdoor activities centered on camping outings, has always been intended to develop resourcefulness in boys.

In the 1960s the sexual revolution, anti-Vietnam War activism, and opposition to government authority fused into a widespread and highly vocal challenge to all kinds of authority. Scouting has taught—and does to this day—respect for authority in the form of parents, teachers, clergy, and duly elected officials. It recognizes the obvious: these people did not acquire their authority by proclamation, tyranny, or the point of a gun. They acquired it by experience, training, and, in the case of government officials, election. A society without order, structure, and respect for legitimate authority devolves into anarchy.

The fringes of our body politic still contain elements of anarchism. More widely, some aspects of the "anti-establishment" movement of the 1960s have metamorphosed into an overemphasis on individualism. Instant gratification and self-absorption seem to be glorified.

Scouting has never been about those things, but about building self-esteem through setting goals and meeting them, working individually and with others. Scouting's "Big Idea"—from the beginning—can be described in one compound word: character-building.

Everything the BSA does is geared toward building character within its members. Through its many ranks and awards, it helps young men set a goal and teaches them that the road to success is often long and arduous. Subsequently, Scouts that fulfill their goals only do so because of resourcefulness and perseverance. This builds confidence, leadership experience, and self-esteem—something that the modern self-esteem movement tries to grant to young people through coddling rather than discipline.

I am reminded of the whole math movement when I think about how liberals value the preservation of self-esteem above all else, including the building of character. With whole math, two plus two doesn't have to equal four. It can equal four, forty, or four hundred, because getting the answer right is not nearly as important as making children feel good. This façade of success gives young people a structure built upon a weak foundation. If such a child, upon becoming an adult and entering the work world as a CPA, carries with him or her the lessons of whole math, then providing wrong information to their clients is accepted. Such children grow to be like a house built on shifting sand, unprepared for the harsh reality of the real world. Esteem must be built on the development of character, and character on the development of discipline.

Like most organizations in the United States, Scouting has a mission statement: "The mission of the Boy Scouts of America is to prepare young people to make ethical and moral choices over their lifetimes by instilling in them the values of the Scout Oath and Law.

Repeated from above, these values are

The Scout Oath: On my honor I will do my best to do my duty to God and my country and to obey the Scout Law; to help other people at all times; to keep myself physically strong, mentally awake, and morally straight.

The Scout Law: A Scout is trustworthy, loyal, helpful, friendly, courteous, kind, obedient, cheerful, thrifty, brave, clean, and reverent.

Does that sound old-fashioned in this modern era? Perhaps, but the best values are the ones that have stood the test of time. And over nearly a century, millions of young men have discovered why.

The Boy Scout Handbook

Now in its eleventh edition (1998), the *Handbook* is the one indispensable guide to Scouting. Its seven sections are "Scouting—The Ultimate Adventure" (an introduction to how Scouting is organized through the patrol and troop); "Climbing to New Heights" (what it takes to work through the various ranks of Scouting); "Scouting's Skills—Ready for the Great Outdoors" (with sections on Hiking, Camping and Cooking); "Scout Service: Doing Your Part" (First Aid, Citizenship); "Personal Development—Prepared for Life" (Making the Most of Yourself, Getting Along with Others, Physically Strong); "Adventure and Opportunity" (Outdoor Adventures, Awards and Recognitions, Opportunities for Older Scouts); and "History of the Boy Scouts of America." Combining all eleven editions, nearly forty million copies of the *Handbook* have been sold, placing it in third place for total sales among copyrighted books. After a few years in Scouting, a boy's 472-page *Handbook* will be well worn, dog-eared, and contain plenty of margin notes.

Cub Scout Division

Although a boy may begin in Boy Scouts at age eleven, many have already gone through the Cub Scout program, which is for boys in the first through fifth grades of school. In Britain, Baden-Powell founded Cub Scouting. In 1930, the BSA added Cub Scouting to its program, validating the vision of Ernest Thompson Seton, whose idea for involvement by younger boys was previously rejected.

Like the Boy Scouts, the Cubs have a graduated program of goals for achieving success. At each level a boy learns skills to move toward his goal. The levels of Cub Scouting are Tiger Cub, Bobcat, Wolf, Bear, and Webelos (a contraction of "We'll be loyal Scouts").

Boy Scout Division

By age eleven, or when a ten-year-old completes the fifth grade or has earned the Webelos's Arrow of Light award, he may become a Scout. At first he holds the rank of Scout. He then earns his way to Tenderfoot. From there, depending upon meeting the requirements of each, he may advance, in order, through Second Class, First Class, Star, Life, and Eagle. Specific requirements for each rank have changed from time to time.

Within the first three ranks, boys advance by demonstrating their abilities in activities involving camping, conservation, cooking, the environment, first aid, hiking, physical fitness, swimming, citizenship, community living, communications, and family living.

Once a boy has reached the rank of First Class, he may work toward Star by earning six merit badges. The next rank, Life, requires five more, and Eagle, the highest rank, requires a total of twenty-one. Each of these ranks has additional requirements.

Eagle Scout

The first Eagle Scout award was earned in 1912. Since then, 1.9 million Eagles have been awarded. As one of those 1.9 million, I can say that the day I received my Eagle at a Court of Honor remains an indelible memory. As any other Eagle can tell you, it is a lot of work, but well worth it. That day, I felt as if I were floating on a cloud. Forty years later, on the exact same day, I was one proud dad when my son received his Eagle, as attaining the goal was not without its trying moments. At age fifteen, Griffin, an avid baseball player, had finished all his merit badge requirements and lacked only his leadership school and Eagle project to finish his quest. Two harrowing years later, with much cajoling and carping from his mom and dad, he overcame the lure of baseball and the dreaded "fumes" to proudly become an Eagle Scout.

Scouting offers 121 merit badges from which boys may choose to hone their skills. Of the 21 the prospective Eagle must earn, 12 are mandatory: First Aid, Citizenship in the Community, Citizenship in the Nation, Citizenship in the World, Communications, Environmental Science, Personal Fitness, Personal Management,

Camping, and Family Life. In addition, he has two elective clusters, choosing between Emergency Preparedness and Lifesaving and one of the following three: Cycling, Hiking, and Swimming.

To reach Eagle, a boy must also design, organize, and carry out a special public service project. At a recent Court of Honor in Eureka, California, three boys were awarded their Eagle badges. Their special projects were typical: Vance Langer supervised the construction and installation of new benches for the public on Bureau of Land Management property. Keith Arnold organized several Scouts and other youths to undertake a massive riverbank cleanup. Brian Butler organized the building of a fence and a picnic area in a city park.

On the way to attaining the rank of Eagle, a Scout learns invaluable first aid techniques. Thanks to his Scout training, one Eagle Scout probably saved his own life when a deranged gunman went on a shooting rampage at Virginia Polytechnic Institute and State University (Virginia Tech) on April 16, 2007. The gunman killed thirty-one students and faculty members, then took his own life. Fifteen others were wounded. According to a news report, Dr. David Stoeckle of Montgomery Regional Hospital in Virginia Tech's hometown of Blacksburg said one student wrapped an electrical cord around his thigh after he was shot in the femoral artery. "The student, a former Eagle Scout, knew he would not survive if he couldn't get the bleeding under control," Stoeckle said (*CBC News*, 5:31 p.m. ET, 17 April 2007).

Scouts with Disabilities

A boy with disabilities can attain Eagle. First, he earns as many required merit badges as possible. Then he submits an application for alternate merit badges. His local Scout Council then settles on the alternate badge program for him.

Eagle Is for Life

The Eagle award lasts a lifetime: once an Eagle Scout, always an Eagle Scout. The National Eagle Scout Association keeps track of its "alumni" wherever life takes them. Eagles have pioneered in many areas: Olympic champions, scientists, physicians, business leaders, elected officials, and senior government officials—to name a few categories.

To paint a picture of purity among all Eagle Scouts would of course be erroneous. That would be the equivalent of saying that once a person becomes a Christian, sin is no longer an issue. One Eagle from my home county of Haskell ended up on death row in Texas.

By and large, though, Eagles demonstrate refined character because they have been tested and developed discipline and confidence that can only come from achievement in the midst of difficult circumstances.

Working Toward Leadership

An assumption of the Scouting program is that every boy will work toward a leadership position. From the first class rank on, the Scout must show his leadership skills by holding a specific youth leadership position in his troop.

The scoutmaster holds a conference with each boy when he is ready to advance in rank. In these conferences, the boy sets his own goals for the next step, with the advice and counsel of the scoutmaster who evaluates his accomplishments in reaching the level just completed. Often the scoutmaster is a father of one of the boys in the troop, but this is by no means a requirement. Indeed, it may be a mother, for in 1988, the BSA opened adult leadership positions to women. Often, a young adult who is a former Scout, enthusiastic to give something back to Scouting, will take on one of the adult leadership positions.

Venturing and Varsity Scouting

From its early days, Scouting has worked to develop programs to keep older boys involved in Scouting. Initially these programs, for boys who had reached age eighteen, were set up as special patrols within the troop and called the Explorer program (often Sea Scouts). Later it was renamed Senior Scouting. In 1972, the older-boy program became the Leadership Corps. Today, older Scouts (to age eighteen) are placed in

Venture patrols. Many of them choose to join Venturing, to which they can belong until they are twenty-one.

Varsity Scouting, a sports-oriented program, is a part of Boy Scouting. It began in 1984 as a program separate from Troop-centered Scouting. The Mormon Church first developed the idea to stem the dropout rate from its Explorer posts. The BSA took it on in 1989 as a program option for older Scouts with varsity teams. The Varsity program uses sports terminology: "squad" for "patrol," "team" for "troop," "coach" for "scoutmaster," and "captain" for "senior patrol leader."

"High Adventure" and Jamborees

The BSA maintains facilities for "High Adventure" activities for Scout groups. Philmont Scout Ranch, with access to more than 200 square miles in New Mexico, offers backpacking treks, horseback "cavalcades," and training and service programs. The Philmont Training Center hosts courses and seminars for Scouting adults.

Northern Tier National High Adventure Bases are operated from facilities in Ely, Minnesota, and offer wilderness canoeing treks from June to September and a special cold-weather camping program, Okpik, beginning in mid-December.

The Florida National High Adventure Sea Base is located in the Florida Keys at Islamorada. It has a variety of programs such as tall ship sailing, coral reef sailing, SCUBA diving training and certification, and Florida fishing and sea exploring. In addition, the facility is used for youth and adult Scouting conferences. One of my closest friends, David Weeks – whose son Elliott received his Eagle at the same Court of Honor Ceremony where my son Griffin received his – was a Sea Scout despite growing up on the dry plains of Abilene, Texas, which shows the nationwide appeal some of these Scout programs have with young men.

The BSA National Council oversees organization of the quadrennial National Scout Jamboree. The first one was held in Washington, D.C., in 1937. Since 1981 the Jamboree has been held at Fort A. P. Hill in Central Virginia.

An individual Scout applies to his local Scout Council to join a Jamboree Troop (or troops in the case of large councils). For ten consecutive days, the jamboree brings together thousands of active Scouts from all over the United States. Side trips take many of the Scouts to historically famous places. In chapter one, I mentioned the thrill I had as a Boy Scout while attending a Jamboree at Valley Forge. Then-president Lyndon Johnson landed there in a helicopter, and the Jamboree also welcomed Lady Olave Baden-Powell, widow of Scouting's founder (and the person who originally proposed the term "jamborese" for such gatherings). How these events—national celebrations—could become fodder for the radical left's attack on the Scouting movement is beyond what most folks can fathom.

As we'll see in later chapters, the national jamboree has become a major issue in the courts involving legal action to include the suing of the Defense Department. Current Secretary of Defense and fellow Eagle Scout Robert Gates, who graciously consented to be interviewed for this book, could not even comment on this aspect of his job due to pending litigation.

Order of the Arrow

Order of the Arrow is Scouting's national Brotherhood of Honor Campers. According to the BSA, the order had 183,000 members at the end of 2006. Members are chosen because they appear to best exemplify the Scout Oath and Scout Law in their daily lives. "Arrowmen," as they are called, are avid about Scouting and promote summer camps, camporees, and year-round camping.

My induction into the Order of the Arrow (OA) happened in summer 1964. The ceremony recognizing the honor campers is called a tap-out. During the campfire at the end of the weeklong regular camp, the OA chief walks among all the campers and dramatically recognizes and "taps the shoulder" of the honorees, who are then led silently out of the campfire area to spend the night alone with only their thoughts. The next morning, the chosen Scouts are collected for briefing on what to expect to finalize their OA membership. This usually is a long weekend encampment that requires rigorous duties and labors. The other ranks in OA are Brotherhood and Vigil. My advancement to Brotherhood occurred the following summer, in 1965.

The Good Turn Program

The concept of individual Scouts performing daily good turns grew quickly into an annual all-Scout event. The first, in 1912, was promotion of a "safe and sane" Fourth of July. Other examples include these: In 1921, Scouts gave aid to flood victims in Pueblo, Colorado, and San Antonio, Texas. In 1934, Scouts collected two million items of clothing, food, and supplies for people in need during the Depression. In 1954, a National Conservation Good Turn saw them distribute 6.2 million trees and 55,000 bird-nesting boxes, and set up 41,000 conservation displays. In 1986, 600,000 Scouts distributed 14 million brochures promoting organ donation.

Since 2004, the BSA's Good Turn for America has been launched in conjunction with the Salvation Army, the American Red Cross, and Habitat for Humanity to address the problems of hunger, homelessness, housing, and poor health.

The Church of Latter-day Saints of Jesus Christ and Scouting

Many churches endorse the Scouting program, and many offer facilities for Scout meetings. (The efforts by Scouting's adversaries to stop this practice will be discussed in chapter five.) However, the Church of Jesus Christ of Latter Day Saints (LDS), widely called the Mormon Church, was the first to adopt Scouting as an official church program for its young members. LDS troops link a boy's Scouting progression with his progression within the church. A Mormon boy must be twelve before entering Scouting (eleven-year-olds have a limited camping program). It is more than a little ironic that in Utah, one of the strongest states in the nation in support of Scouting, the Scouts were apparently banned from helping with the 2002 Winter Olympics. Even with Mitt Romney, a fellow Eagle Scout, serving as president of the Olympic Games, the local Scout leaders were kept out of the games as volunteers. I will comment on this further.

Scouting as a "Grassroots" Organization

Scouting is a "grassroots" movement because its strength begins with its smallest unit, the patrol. In a chart, the Scouting movement's organization would look like a pyramid, with the patrol at the top. As you move down from the top, the pyramid grows ever larger, from the troop, to the troop committee, the district, council, area, and region until it reaches the National Council at the bottom.

The basic unit, the patrol, is typically eight in number. It gives a boy real-time experience in teamwork. It provides early opportunities for him to take responsibility and carry out projects. The boys in the patrol elect their own Patrol Leader. Together, all of the troop's Patrol Leaders make up the Patrol Leader Council. The entire troop elects the Senior Patrol Leader (SPL). He then appoints as many Assistant Senior Patrol Leaders (ASPL) as the size of the troop warrants.

The troop is made up of as many patrols as the number of boys warrants. For example, if there are forty-eight boys and eight is considered optimum for a patrol, there will be six patrols. A guiding principle of Scouting is that it is "boy-run." As one active assistant scoutmaster told me recently, "Boys learn by making mistakes. You might call it 'controlled failure.'" It's how they instill the leadership skills to make Scouting a long-lasting, positive influence on the boys.

The Senior Patrol Leader actually runs the troop, with the advice and counsel of the adult leadership, consisting of the scoutmaster and as many assistant scoutmasters as the troop size warrants.

Troops and other Scout units are grouped into districts. Districts are organized by Scout Councils. The nation's smallest council in Piedmont, California, is itself one district because it comprises all the troops in a single small city. In the large nearby Mount Diablo Council, however, there are districts for entire counties or sections of large counties within it. A professional District Executive manages administration of a district.

At the council level, a professional Council Executive oversees administration. Councils, in turn, are grouped into Areas, with each Area having a professional executive. Above that level are Regions

(Northeast, Western, Southern, Central), each of which has a professional executive team.

Finally, there is the National Council, the not-for-profit corporation that was chartered by Congress. It is governed by an elected National Executive Board based at BSA headquarters in Irving, Texas, near Dallas. The Chief Scout Executive, a professional, and his staff manage its day-to-day operations.

Adult Volunteers

Just as the actual programs of Scouting are "boy-run," so the adult supervision is "volunteer-run." Each troop has a Troop Committee. "Civilian" parents and other adults from the community run the committee. A chairman elected by the committee members heads it. It also has a Chartering Organization Representative (COR). Technically, the COR outranks all others because he or she is the link to the troop's chartering organization. Scouting's rules say that without a chartering organization, there can be no troop. The chartering organization may be a religious organization, a service club, a local business, or some other recognized entity. It provides the troop a regular meeting place and other support. The troop committee's role is to see to the troop's "back office" activities such as its treasury, policy, recruiting, youth protection training, and leadership training.

The tenure of adult volunteers varies, of course, but some serve for many years. Gene Yoss of Boulder, Colorado, may have set some sort of record when he logged in his thirty-fourth year as cubmaster of Boulder's Pack 179 not long ago. At age sixty-five, he told the Associated Press, "The kids are great; they just pump me up to the point where I feel I'm thirty years old again." ("After 34 Years, Boulder Resident Still Leads the Pack," Associated Press, 23 January 2003) The Pack 179 committee chairman, Joe Glynn, said of Yoss's mixture of skits, games, songs, flag ceremonies, field trips, and award presentations for the boys, "Boy, does he have that pack running like a fine Swiss watch." With so many activities for boys and girls today, Yoss still said Scouting is one of the best. "It's an attempt to get the parents to listen to their boy when he's young so they don't have to get upset with him in his teens," he says.

The steady hand of dedicated adult volunteers in Scouting can also be a great help to single mothers. According to the Census Bureau's latest report (2005), some 10 million single mothers have children at home under eighteen years of age. The wholesome activities of the Scouts, backed by sympathetic and caring adults as advisors (scoutmasters or assistant scoutmasters) means that sons of single mothers can find admirable role models as they enter the difficult years of adolescence.

Organization Beyond the Troop

Districts, Councils, Areas, and Regions all have similar committees made up of volunteer community leaders. In each case, the professional executive reports to them. At the national level, there is a sixty-five-member National Executive Board. Its members are elected for one-year terms, but there is no limit to the number of terms one may serve. Most retire by the time they reach their mid-sixties, often moving on to the Advisory Council.

The board elects the president for a one-year term from among its members. The executive board is similar in its functions to that of a company. It sets policy and hires the Chief Scout Executive, who reports to the board. Recently, to replace the retiring Chief Scout Executive (in effect, Scouting's Chief Executive Officer), the board went through the process of choosing a new one from among six finalists. It has five standing committees: Administration Group, Program Group, Human Resources Group, Regional Presidents' Group, and Relationships & Marketing Group.

When you add it all together, Scouting is a sizable organization. At the end of 2006, 4,619,730 youths participated in Cub Scouting, Boy Scouting, Venturing, and Learning-for-Life programs. In addition, 1,190,992 adults volunteered and 137,884 total units and groups existed from coast to coast ("BSA 2006 Annual Report, "Combined Traditional Membership/Participation Totals," scouting.org/media/reports/2006/11mentotals.html). Add to that the number of boys who have gone through Scouting's programs in nearly a century, and the grand total is approximately100 million.

The Culture War
Comes to Scouting

David Park joined the Boy Scouts of America on March 1, 1976. He was and is a one-man legal department. At that time he was aware of a lawsuit that had been working its way through the courts for some time: *Schwenk vs. Boy Scouts of America.*

The "Schwenk" in the suit was Carla Schwenk, a nine-year-old girl from Portland, Oregon, who had been turned down for membership in a Cub Scout Pack. The lawsuit, brought by her mother, Roberta, alleged that the BSA's refusal to allow Carla membership in the Cub Scouts was discriminatory and in violation of state law. Looking back some thirty-one years later, Park, who is still National Counsel of the BSA, says it was the first "shot across the bow" in what would become a long-running volley of lawsuits challenging Scouting's traditions and its right to keep those traditions into the future. Some have called this an assault on the Boy Scouts; others see it as part of a much larger phenomenon, a "culture war" between determined secularists and the traditional values of American society. It is all of the above.

In all, the Boy Scouts have been involved in thirty lawsuits since the filing of the Schwenk case. The suits fall into four categories:

• Girls seeking membership in the BSA;
• Scouting's "duty to God";
• Scouting's duty to be "morally straight"; and
• Scouting's access to "government forums."

The first three categories involve Scouting's membership standards. The BSA's first line of defense was that "public accommodation" laws did not apply to it as a private organization. As such, their acknowledgment of God in the Scout Oath and their refusal to permit openly gay scoutmasters are constitutionally protected expressions of free speech and free association. Over the years, the BSA has often asserted that the First Amendment protects the Scout Oath and Law as forms of free speech.

Discrimination against Girls?

Schwenk vs. Boy Scouts of America contended that the BSA had violated Oregon's public accommodation law by denying Carla membership in the Cub Scouts. The Scouts' lawyers filed a demurrer, in effect, asking the court to set aside the case because, they said, the plaintiff "failed to state a cause of action" (Oregon State Supreme Court decision, 24 June 1976).

The local Circuit Court for Multnomah County granted the Scouts' demurrer, but that was not the end of the case. The Schwenks then took it to the state court of appeals. The demurrer was sustained, but the Schwenks took it to the final level, the State Supreme Court, which, after hearing the case, affirmed the earlier rulings on June 26, 1976. There are several other cases involving girls' efforts to join the Boy Scouts:

• *Mankes vs. Boy Scouts of America.* In 1991, the parents of eight-year-old Margot Mankes sued the BSA because she had been turned down for membership in Dade County, Florida's Cub Pack 350 and in a Scout summer camp scheduled to begin June 24 of that year. They asked that the Federal District Court rule that the Scouts were in violation of state and local laws. They also asked for an injunction requiring the Scouts to admit Margot into the pack and to attend the summer camp. The federal court dismissed the case because it did not have jurisdiction to hear it.

In its ruling, however, the court noted,

Plaintiff asserts that the Boy Scouts membership requirement, which restricts membership to boys, results in sex discrimination. . . . The Boy Scouts' goals to instill the ideals of leadership, self-confidence and moral character are not new. The goals to ease transition of boys from youth to adulthood have remained constant, and were the basis for the Congressional charter as an organization for boys. It should be clear that the Court is not sending a message to plaintiff that she must settle for participation in the Girl Scouts, but that there is nothing inherently discriminatory about the Boys Scouts' goals. The Boy Scouts did not, in creating its organization to help develop the moral character of young boys, intentionally set out to discriminate against girls.

• *Department of Human Rights (Minnesota) vs. Boy Scouts of America.* On behalf of Clare Bicknese, a thirteen-year-old girl who wanted to join Troop 394 of the Dan Patch District of the Viking Council of the Boy Scouts, the state's Human Rights Commission sought an injunction in May 1992 to prohibit the Scouts from refusing her membership. The state's Fourth Judicial District Court for Hennepin County heard the case.

The Human Rights Commission argued that the Scouts were in violation of the state's Human Rights Act. Also, they claimed that Clare's father, an adult leader in the Boy Scouts, would supervise her merit badge work. The father, Dean Bicknese, was at the time the Advancement Chairman of Troop 394 and Activities Chairman of the Dan Patch District of the Viking Council.

Nevertheless, the court denied the petition for an injunction. It said, "To hold that the Minnesota Human Rights Act compels the Boy Scouts of America to admit girls as members would violate both the Minnesota and Unites States Constitutions' freedom-of-association provisions." It added, "If Congress would have intended that girls be allowed in the Boy Scouts and vice versa, it would have chartered one organization, i.e., Scouts of America." (Congress chartered Boy Scouts and Girl Scouts separately within a few years of each other.)

The court cited two other reasons for denying the petition: "The Minnesota Human Rights Act is inapplicable to the Boy Scouts of America because that organization is exempt from the Act by virtue of not being a 'public accommodation'; and the Boy Scouts of America is an educational institution and the Minnesota Human Rights Act specifically permits educational institutions to limit themselves to one sex."

• *Yeaw vs. Boy Scouts of America.* Eleven-year-old Katrina Yeaw's twin brother was a Boy Scout. She wanted to be one, too. After Troop 349 of California's Golden Empire Council turned down her membership application, her father took the Scouts to court, seeking an injunction to require them to admit her. His suit claimed that the Boy Scouts was a "business establishment" as defined by the state's Unruh Civil Rights Act and was therefore prohibited from discriminating against girls by denying them membership.

The Sacramento County Superior Court denied the Yeaws' request for an injunction. The family then went to the state's Court of Appeals. On June 2, 1997, the appellate court upheld the lower court in ruling that ". . . the Boy Scouts is not a business establishment within the meaning of the [Unruh] Act. Accordingly, the Boy Scouts may lawfully exclude females from membership in its ranks."

In its ruling the court noted, "Significantly, the Boy Scouts is a membership organization whose benefits derive primarily, if not exclusively, from the interpersonal associations among its members. The relationships in Scouting are gratuitous, continuous, personal, social." It added, "Every boy is, first and foremost, part of a patrol, a group of three-to-eight boys within a Troop. Each patrol has its own name, its own badge, its own meetings, its own elected leaders, and its own sense of identity. The members lead, plan and organize their own activities, thereby gaining skills in leadership, planning, and cooperation. The patrol becomes a close knit group of boys who have learned to provide for each other's personal needs."

One case involved a woman who wanted to become a scoutmaster. Historically, particular positions of adult leadership of Scouting units (scoutmaster, assistant scoutmaster, and Webelos leaders) had been exclusively male. "Leadership Qualifications," an article in the spring 1988 issue of *BSA Today*, described the reasoning for this policy: "The long-standing tradition of providing exclusively male leadership to adolescent boys in Boy Scouting was rooted in the belief that a crucial part of a boy's development as he grows older is his relationship with a caring adult male. Scouting has provided a structure in which men can interact with boys in a non-threatening way, more as friends or mentors than as authority figures."

Catherine N. Pollard challenged this policy. In 1971 no man could be found to volunteer to serve as scoutmaster of Connecticut's Troop 13. Mrs. Pollard became, in effect, the scoutmaster. She was the *de facto* leader for five years. In 1974 and again in 1976 she attempted to register officially as the scoutmaster. Both times her request was turned down. She then filed a complaint of sex discrimination with the Connecticut Commission on Human Rights and Opportunities. On filing the complaint, she had to step down as the troop's leader; however, once again no man could be found to lead Troop 13, so it was forced to disband.

In 1984 the Connecticut Commission ruled that the BSA had violated the state's public accommodation law and must register Mrs. Pollard as a scoutmaster. The BSA immediately filed suit against the commission, challenging the ruling (*Quinnipiac Council vs. Commission on Human Rights & Opportunities*). In 1986, a Superior Court struck down the commission's ruling, accepting the BSA's arguments. The crux of these was that, while young Cub Scouts and Explorer Posts' older Scouts could be led by women, ten-year-old boys in Webelos and those in Scout troops (ages 11-17) needed a male role model to look up to "in the difficult process of maturing to adulthood."

The commission appealed the ruling, and the state's Supreme Court on July 6, 1987, upheld that ruling.

At about that time, the BSA was also reconsidering its all-male leader policy. The number of one-parent households was increasing throughout the country, and most were single-mother households. On February 11, 1988, the BSA National Executive Board voted unanimously to remove gender requirements for all adult leadership positions.

The spring 1988 article in *BSA Today* noted, "It is time to recognize that in our changing society the unique strength of Scouting lies in the dedicated efforts of both men and women. Our efforts must be focused on helping chartered organizations select the best possible leadership, male or female, to carry forward a Scouting program that serves the youth and adults for whom the organizations are responsible."

Mrs. Pollard, by then a seventy-year-old widow and grandmother, was quoted as saying, "I do think this is marvelous because there have been women all over the United States . . . that have been doing these things for the Boy Scouts because we could not get a male leader" (www.bsa-discrimination.org, accessed 29 May 2007).

There is no reason to believe that there was any connection between these cases. It is possible that news of the filing of one served as encouragement for others thinking of similar action, but the cases were separated in time, often by several years.

Evidence of a planned, strategic assault on the Scouts did not arise until the American Civil Liberties Union (ACLU) became involved, with cases that focused on the reference in the Scout Oath to "duty to God."

The Battles over God

By the early nineties the emphasis of legal challenges to the Boy Scouts began to shift from girls' and women's membership to atheists and agnostics attempting to overturn the "duty to God" element in the Scout Oath and the requirement of the BSA constitution and by-laws that all Scouts affirm belief in God.

In 1981, the leadership of the American Civil Liberties Union apparently decided to test the ability of the Boy Scouts to maintain its membership criteria. Its ACLU Foundation of Southern California, a regional affiliate of the national ACLU, represented a gay activist in a case against the BSA.

It was not until the 1991 *Randall* case involving the Scouts' "duty to God" requirement, however, that the BSA believed the ACLU had decided to make it the target of a determined strategy to overturn the basis for its membership rules. The ACLU, which prided itself on its long history of rights protection, had a checkered beginning. One of its founders was Elizabeth Gurley Flynn, a leader of the Communist Party U.S.A. during the thirties. In 1940, on the heels of the nefarious

Stalin-Hitler pact, the true civil libertarians in the ACLU managed to oust Flynn and focus the group on its basic mission.

More difficulties lay ahead, however. In 1968, in a New York teachers' strike in which black revolutionaries figured, the head of the ACLU's New York chapter sided with the radicals over the teachers. Ever since, there have been periodic tugs-of-war within the organization—between earnest civil libertarians and members with an ultra-leftist agenda.

Getting God out of public life has been a major goal of the ACLU for a quarter of a century or longer. It has initiated or threatened lawsuits against numerous cities, counties, and schools to remove any references to God in ceremonies or displays. This has extended to Christmas. The ACLU was successful in getting school prayers banned in the 1960s. A recent case before the U. S. Ninth Circuit, though narrow in jurisdiction, resulted in the Pledge of Allegiance being banned because of its phrase, "one nation under God."

The BSA offered a tempting target to the ACLU. After all, its bylaws state, "the Boy Scouts of America maintains that no member can grow into the best kind of citizen without recognizing an obligation to God." Presumably even more egregious in the eyes of ACLU lawyers was Scouting's explicit directions to members at various levels in Scouting, found in *The Boy Scout Handbook* (11th ed., Irving, Texas: Boy Scouts of America, 1998). For example, a Bobcat Cub Scout ". . . is required to promise to do his best to do his 'duty to God,' which means 'Put God first.' Do what you know God wants you to do." A Wolf Cub Scout is required to ". . . talk with your folks about what they believe is their duty to God. Give some ideas on how you can practice or demonstrate your religious beliefs, and find out how you can help your church, synagogue, or religious fellowship."

The intensity of commitment increases as a boy moves up the ladder of Scouting. For a Bear Cub Scout it is ". . . practice your religion as you are taught in your home, church, synagogue, mosque, or other religious community." For a Webelos Scout (the transitional step to Boy Scouts) it is "Earn the religious emblem of your faith or do two of the following: Attend church, synagogue, mosque, or other religious organization of your choice, talk with your religious leader about your beliefs, and tell your family and Webelos den leader about what you learned." Or "Tell how your religious beliefs fit in with the Scout Oath and Scout Law. Discuss this with your family and Webelos den leader: What character-building traits do your beliefs and the Scout Oath and Scout Law have in common?"

Second Class, First Class, Star, Life, and Eagle Scouts are ". . . required to demonstrate Scout spirit by living the Scout Oath . . . and Scout Law in your everyday life."

Volunteer adult leaders also are expected "to do their duty to God and be reverent as embodied in the Scout Oath, the Scout Law and the Declaration of Religious Principle." Scouting, therefore, does not accept atheists and agnostics as adult leaders.

From its earliest days, Scouting has welcomed boys of varying religious faiths. The one thing they have in common is belief in a supreme being.

The ACLU was not involved in the first of the "duty to God" cases, *Welsh vs. Boy Scouts of America.* The plaintiffs in the case were Elliott Welsh and his seven-year-old son, Mark, of Hinsdale, Illinois, who claimed to be agnostics and refused to affirm a belief in God. The father wanted Mark to be a Tiger Cub Scout, and he wanted to be the adult partner of his son. The case was brought in the U.S. District Court for the Northern District of Illinois in 1990. The Welshes contended that the BSA was "a place of public accommodation" and that it practiced unlawful discrimination under Title II of the Civil Rights Act of 1964. The District Court ruled that the BSA was not a "place of public accommodation."

The Welshes appealed to the 7th Circuit of the U.S. Court of Appeals, which upheld the District Court's decision, ruling that the BSA was not a "place of public accommodation" for purposes of Title II and that even if it were, Scouting would fall within the "private club" exception to Title II.

Next was the case of Michael and William Randall, twin brothers who had joined a Cub Scout pack in Culver City (Los Angeles County), California, when they were seven years of age. They advanced from Tiger to Bobcat to Wolf rank in Cubs. Later, in the trial of *Randall vs. Orange County Council,* Boy Scouts of America, the boys testified that they were not asked to repeat the Cub Scout Promise often, and when they were they omitted the word "God." Also, when they told their Cub den leader they did not believe in God, he allowed them to omit the reference. The den leader testified to the contrary, saying that the boys had recited the entire promise and had not raised any question about the inclusion of "God" in the recitation.

After a time, the Randall family moved to Anaheim Hills in Orange County. The boys joined Cub Scout Den 4 of Pack 519. They worked on advancement to Bear rank, which (as noted earlier in this chapter) has a specific religious component. A boy seeking Bear rank is instructed to ". . . practice your religion as you are taught in your home, church, synagogue, mosque or other religious community." Since this was not the case with the Randall twins, they were told they could not advance. The Orange County Council of the BSA took the position that, under the circumstances, they could not even participate in Cub Scouts.

The boys, through their mother, filed a complaint on February 18, 1991, with the Orange County Superior Court seeking—and get-ting—a preliminary injunction that barred the exclusion of the boys from the Cub Scouts program. Shortly after the complaint was filed, the ACLU Foundation of Southern California became involved in the representation of the boys' case. The boys' father, James Grafton Randall, was their original lawyer and continued to be actively involved in the case after the ACLU became involved.

The boys' lawyers set out to prove that the Orange County Council operated as a business establishment as defined by California's Unruh Act, which prohibits discrimination in places of business. They also sought to prove that religion plays only a minimal role in the Cub Scout program. They also said that because the Orange County Council accepted funds from the United Way, no individual served by any United Way program could be required to take part in religious activities as a requirement of participation.

The Superior Court ruled in favor of the Randalls and issued a permanent injunction preventing the Scouts from excluding them from membership or advancement in Cubs based upon religious belief (or none at all).

The Scouts appealed the decision, and the Court of Appeal gave a split decision. It ruled that the BSA was a "business establishment" under the Unruh Act; however, since the Cub pack or den had not been named in the suit, the Court reversed the original judgment so far as it concerned the pack and den.

The Scouts then asked for and got a review of the case by the state's Supreme Court. It overturned the decision in favor of the Randalls by concluding that the Boy Scouts were not a "business establishment" under the Unruh Act. Therefore, the Court decided, the BSA could not be required under state law to change its membership criteria. The decision was filed on March 23, 1998, more than seven years after the Randalls' original complaint was filed.

By 2007, the ACLU's involvement in fourteen cases against the Boy Scouts had covered, cumulatively, more than one hundred years of litigation. Coincidentally, the final arguments in the Randall case were heard on the same day the California Supreme Court heard another ACLU case, *Curran vs. Mount Diable Council, Boy Scouts of America* (discussed later in this chapter).

In 1991, another case arose that would end up in court as *Seabourn vs. Coronado Council, Boy Scouts of America*. This one involved an adult volunteer in Scouting, Bradford W. Seabourn, who had served for some seven years as assistant scoutmaster of Troop 76 of the Pawnee District of the Coronado Area Council of the BSA in Manhattan, Kansas.

Beginning as a seven-year-old Cub, he went on to Boy Scouts and reached the level of Life Scout. Presumably he was not an atheist at the time. He attended church and was thought to share the religious beliefs of his parents. If that were true at one time, clearly it was no longer.

In the September 1991 issue of the council's newsletter, the council's president printed a "reaffirmation" statement, "On Duty to God." The BSA had approved the statement.

On September 9, Seabourn wrote to the council to say that he chose to define God as "nothing." He wrote, "When I say the Pledge of Allegiance, I pledge my oath to 'One Nation, under nothing.' When I say the Scout Oath, I promise to 'do my duty, to nothing' and my country. . . . When I say the Scout Law, I say a Scout is reverent to 'nothing.'"

Seabourn was the father of four boys, two of whom were old enough to participate in Scouting. While his letter praised the character-building activities of Scouting, he wrote that the newsletter article "On Duty to God" needed a qualification, "that a belief in a supernatural being is not a necessary requirement for entrance into Scouting, and that respect for others' beliefs included respect for those who lack belief in God (or a god) as well."

Two days after receiving Seabourn's letter, the Coronado Area Council denied his registration as an adult leader. It advised him he could ask for the regional director to review his termination. He did.

On October 16 he wrote to the Assistant Regional Director requesting the review. The lawyerly language of his letter suggests that even then he was preparing for a legal challenge. He described his termination as "entirely pernicious and arbitrary in nature, completely irresponsible and uninformed in its origin, and demonstrat[ed] partiality and discrimination against [his] religious viewpoints."

On November 12, the Assistant Regional Director wrote to Seabourn, upholding the denial of Seabourn's registration. On December 11, Seabourn wrote to the Chief Scout Executive, asking for a review by Scouting's National Executive Board.

In February 1992, while this was pending, Seabourn wrote the board asking for a complimentary adult registration or waiver of the registration requirement in order to accompany his fifteen-year-old son to Philmont Scout Ranch for a two-week High Adventure trip in mid-July. In April, this request was denied.

Seabourn next asked the Kansas Human Rights Commission for a restraining order against the Boy Scouts. Seabourn contended that the BSA's denial of his request to go to Philmont with his son violated the "public accommodations" section of the Kansas Act Against Discrimination on the basis of religious discrimination. On June 29, the chief legal council of the commission advised Seabourn that it had no statutory authority in such cases.

Thwarted once again, Seabourn filed, on July 9, a motion in Riley County District Court for a temporary restraining order to enjoin the Boy Scouts from preventing him in accompanying his son on the Philmont trip. The next day, the court denied his motion.

In September, Seabourn filed suit against the Coronado Area Council under the Kansas Act Against Discrimination. The Boy Scouts filed a motion for summary—that is, immediate—judgment. The Riley County District Court granted the motion. As in many other cases, it ruled that the Boys Scouts do not constitute a "public accommodation."

Bradford Seabourn continued his efforts to be reinstated despite his declared atheism. He appealed the case to the highest state court, the Kansas Supreme Court. In 1995 it ruled as the lower court had done, that the BSA is not a "public accommodation" within the meaning of the state's Act Against Discrimination and that Kansas law couldn't force the Scouts to change their "duty to God" requirements for adult leaders. Its ruling stated, "The record supports our conclusion that the Boy Scouts has no business purpose other than maintaining the objectives and programs to which the operation of facilities is merely incidental."

In December 1992, Margaret Downey-Schottmiller, an atheist, filed a complaint against the Boy Scouts with the Pennsylvania Human Rights Commission. She had applied to become a volunteer adult leader, but was denied because she refused to abide by the requirement in the Scout Oath requiring her to affirm that she would do her "duty to God."

After a hearing, the commission dismissed her complaint on the ground that the local Scout Council was not a "public accommodation." She turned to the ACLU of Pennsylvania, an affiliate of the national organization. It represented her in an appeal (*Downey-Schottmiller vs. Commonwealth of Pennsylvania Human Relations Commission*). On July 13, 2000, she agreed to dismiss the appeal in light of the landmark U.S. Supreme Court's landmark decision in June (that case will be discussed later in this chapter).

The Downey-Schottmiller case was the last one based explicitly on "duty to God" requirements for membership by boys and adults in the

Boy Scout organization. It was not the end of lawsuits—by a long shot. Next came a cluster of suits that challenged another Scout membership requirement.

"Morally Straight"—What Does It Mean?

BSA units do not routinely ask a prospective adult leader about his (or her) sex life. The organization takes the position that this subject is a private matter and certainly not part of any Scout program.

In the Scout Oath, the boy promises to be "morally straight." In the Scout Law, he promises to be "clean." What do these phrases mean? The *Boy Scout Handbook* says that to be "morally straight" is "to be a person of strong character . . . your relationships with others should be honest and open. You should respect and defend the rights of all people. Be clean in your speech and actions, and remain faithful in your religious beliefs. The values you practice as a Scout will help you shape a life of virtue and self-reliance."

"Clean" is explained this way: "A Scout keeps his body and mind fit and clean. He chooses the company of those who live by high standards. He helps keep his home and community clean." The word "straight" was used in this context long before it took on the definition of "heterosexual" and before "gay" became a synonym for "homosexual."

The BSA's position is that a homosexual who makes his sex life a public matter is not an appropriate role model of the Scout Oath and Law for adolescent boys. Many agree with this assessment; others disagree.

I do not believe the teaching of sexual preference fits within the parameters of Scouting's mission. The defining characteristic of homosexuality and heterosexuality is sex. Scouting is not intended to advance a discussion about sexual activity, whether of the heterosexual form or the homosexual form.

You will find few parents of Scouts concerned about the homosexual scoutmaster whose sexuality is not disclosed as long as sexuality in no way enters into the scout-scoutmaster relationship.

One of Scouting's wise policies that other organizations have since adopted is the two-deep policy. This requires that another adult always be present during interaction between a Scout and an adult Scout leader. This not only protects the youth, but the adult (from all manner of accusation).

We would no more want an adult Scout leader talking about his heterosexual exploits in front of young Scouts than we would homosexual activity. The point is that Scouting is not the place for sex education. When a gay or lesbian leader makes an issue of his or sexual preference, it makes it impossible to remove sexual conduct from the Scouting realm.

Though I am no expert on the "nature versus nurture" debate, I can sympathize with those who believe sexual preference is genetic. It may be so, but it remains unproved. Even if it were, this does not mean we are ultimately not responsible for the active choices we make. Even if an alcoholic is powerless over alcohol once it enters his body, he still makes a choice to drink. And, even if someone is attracted to a person of the same sex, he or she still makes a choice to engage in sexual activity with someone of the same gender.

A loving, tolerant view toward those who have a different sexual preference is the ideal position—for both the heterosexual and the homosexual. I do not believe in condemning homosexuals that I know personally. I believe in valuing their lives like any others, as our God in heaven does. Tolerance, however, should not only be asked of the proponents of traditional values. The radical homosexual movement seeks societal normalization of their sexual activity. I respect their right to engage in the individual behavior of their choosing, but they must respect the right of millions in society to refuse to normalize their behavior.

The issue as it applies to Scouting is not so much the gay scoutmaster who keeps his consentual sexual activity confined to the bedroom, but the agenda of radical gay rights groups that want to throw their sexual activity into the face of society, despite the decision by millions of families not to teach the gay lifestyle as an acceptable alternative.

Tolerance is a two-way street. The Boy Scouts is not the proper intersection for a debate over sexual preference.

A number of active homosexuals, with the assistance of the ACLU and a chorus of support from various gay activist organizations, have challenged the BSA's long-standing policy. They have filed lawsuits alleging unfair discrimination. This effort received the attention of the U.S. Supreme Court in 2000. Nearly twenty years before that, the first challenge began with the case of *Curran vs. Mount Diablo Council, Boy Scouts of America*. The national ACLU's regional affiliate, the ACLU Foundation of Southern California, represented Timothy Curran, the plaintiff, throughout the course of the litigation.

Tim Curran, who was openly homosexual, applied to the Mount Diablo Council in northern California to be an adult Scout leader. He was turned down. With the ACLU as his legal counsel, he filed suit on April 22, 1981, alleging discrimination. After a trial in the Los Angeles County Superior Court, the court ruled in favor of the Scouts. The Court of Appeals affirmed the trial court's ruling 2 to 1; however, the state Supreme Court granted a review of the case. It concluded unanimously that the BSA is not a "business establishment" under the Unruh Civil Rights Act's requirement of equal rights to public accommodations. The final ruling took place on March 23, 1988, nearly seven years after the initial filing.

In Chicago, G. Keith Richardson, also an open homosexual, filed a claim under Chicago's human rights ordinance against the local Boy Scout Council. His claim: that the council had denied him employment because of his open homosexuality. The Roger Baldwin Foundation of the ACLU of Illinois, the national ACLU's regional affiliate, represented him throughout the litigation that ensued (*Chicago Area Council, Boy Scouts of America vs. City of Chicago Commission on Human Relations*).

Ultimately, an Illinois appeals court held that the Boy Scouts could require a job applicant to observe the Scout Oath and Law when seeking employment as a professional who would be acting as a representative for Scouting. The court asked the Human Rights Commission to determine whether Richardson had been seeking a non-representative position. The commission said he had not. The original complaint was filed in May 1992 and finally resolved in February 2003.

In the District of Columbia, Roland Pool and Michael Geller had applied to become volunteer adult Scout leaders. As open homosexuals, both were turned down. They filed a complaint with the D.C. Commission on Human Rights. The ACLU of the National Capital Area, the national ACLU's regional affiliate, was "of counsel" for them. In June 2001, the commission ruled that the BSA and its National Capital Area Council had violated the District's Human Rights Act of 1977.

The BSA appealed to the District of Columbia Court of Appeals (*Boy Scouts of America vs. District of Columbia Commission on Human Rights*). The Appeals Court reversed the Human Rights Commission, ruling that forcing the Scouts to appoint open homosexuals to leadership positions would violate the BSA's First Amendment right to freedom of "expressive association." (This followed the landmark Dale decision discussed below.)

The Dale Case

The climactic case in this category involved James Dale, an assistant scoutmaster in Monmouth County in central New Jersey. Jim Dale joined the Cubs in 1978, when he was eight years old. He moved on to Scouts and worked up through all the ranks until he attained Eagle. When he turned eighteen he became an assistant scoutmaster.

About the time he began college (Rutgers University in 1989), Dale came to the conclusion that he was gay. As his sophomore year began, he started attending meetings of the student Gay and Lesbian Alliance at Rutgers. A few months later he was elected its president. At that time he was still an assistant scoutmaster.

The following summer, between his sophomore and junior years, he gave a talk to a group of social workers that touched on his sexual orientation. A newspaper account of the meeting came to the attention of his local troop and council. The Monmouth Council of Boy Scouts wrote to him advising that he could no longer be in Scouting because its policy did not permit active homosexuals to participate. Dale insisted that he knew nothing about this aspect of BSA policy.

That may be true, although the policy was no secret, and as a Scout leader he must have had access to printed materials that spelled it out. Nevertheless, one can sympathize with Dale about the inner turmoil he must have gone through as he concluded he was homosexual.

He felt hurt and rejected by the letter. In a July 17, 2000, interview with the online magazine *Salon,* he said, "That letter from the Boy Scouts probably made me more of an activist." (Kera Bolonik, "A Conversation With James Dale," Salon, 17 July 2000.)

In 1990 he decided to sue the Boy Scouts. The ACLU filed friend-of-the-court (*amicus curiae*) briefs at several steps along the way. From the beginning, the Lambda Legal Defense Fund, a gay advocacy law firm, had taken his case at no charge.

In July 1992, he filed suit against the Scouts in the Superior Court of New Jersey, Chancery Division-Monmouth County. His charge was that the Scouts had violated the New Jersey Law Against Discrimination. That law prohibited discrimination in "public accommodations" on the basis of sexual orientation. Nevertheless, the Superior Court granted summary judgment in favor of the Boy Scouts.

Dale appealed the ruling. The New Jersey Appellate Division held that the Boy Scouts had violated the state's public accommodations law. The state Supreme Court upheld that ruling. Then the case moved to the United States Supreme Court (*Boy Scouts of America vs. Dale*). The nation's highest court reversed the New Jersey Supreme Court, 5-4. It said that a state, through its anti-discrimination laws, may not prohibit the Boy Scouts from adhering to a moral point of view and expressing it in internal leadership policy. It said that the New Jersey Supreme Court's decision violated the Boy Scouts' First Amendment right of freedom of association.

Approximately twenty organizations on either side of the case filed *amicus curiae* briefs. It attracted much news media attention as well as hotly expressed opinions in letters to the editor, op-ed columns, talk radio, and television interviews.

Despite Dale's legal challenge to the Boy Scouts, he was not wholly against the organization. He was interviewed in April 1998 by *The Advocate,* a magazine whose audience is largely gay and lesbian.

He was asked, "Growing up, did you find the Scouts to be a homophobic environment?" He replied, "If anything, I think it was much less homophobic than the norm of society. I think the Boy Scouts allows for the human factor a lot more than (do) other organizations." (Benoit Louis-Genizet, "The Model Boy Scout," The Advocate, 14 April 1998.)

The high court's decision in June 2000 effectively ended nearly twenty years of varied legal challenges to Boy Scout membership criteria. There have been none since; however, many more battles in the culture war lay ahead for the Boy Scouts.

Pressure and Intimidation vs. The First Amendment

Even before the Supreme Court's landmark ruling in the Dale case in June 2000, the ACLU and its allies had begun to shift strategy and tactics in their effort to force the Boy Scouts to remake their structure.

Legal challenge after legal challenge to the Scouts had failed. The courts had sided with the Scouts in the matter of girls seeking membership. They had affirmed the Scouts' right to include "duty to God" in the Scout Oath, which every member must affirm. They had upheld the Scouts' right to determine criteria for membership, inasmuch as it is a private organization. This meant the Scouts could continue to deny membership to Scouts or adult leaders who were open/activist homosexuals.

In the late nineties, the ACLU activated a two-pronged strategy to challenge the Boy Scouts' use of school facilities, on the one hand, and to get communities with anti-discrimination ordinances to deny further use of municipal facilities by the Scouts on the grounds that their policy on homosexuals was a violation of those ordinances and constituted "discrimination."

Predating this strategy was a 1992 case in which the ACLU was not involved, *Sherman vs. Community Consolidated School District 21 of Wheeling Township*. In this case, Robert (Rob) and Richard (Ricky) Sherman, an atheist father and son, sued their school district, in a Chicago suburb, claiming that it had violated the clause of the U.S. Constitution prohibiting the establishment of a state religion by allowing the Boy Scouts to use the facilities of an elementary school. The Scouts had distributed literature during school hours and met in school rooms after hours. The District Court and the Seventh Circuit Court of appeals ruled that the school district did not violate the "establishment" clause by allowing the Scouts to use its facilities as they did. The U.S. Supreme Court, in May 1994, refused to take the case for review.

In a similar case in Michigan, *Scalise vs. Boy Scouts of America*, John Scalise, an atheist, and his son, Benjamin, in 2000 sued the Lake Huron Area Council of the Boy Scouts and the Mount Pleasant school board because the Scouts were allowed to use school rooms after hours and to distribute fliers to students during school hours. They contended that the school's policy regarding the Scouts added up to religious discrimination under the state's constitution and its Elliott-Larsen Civil Rights Act. The trial court disagreed, dismissing the Scalises' claim. The Michigan Court of Appeals upheld the lower court. It went all the way to the U.S. Supreme Court, which denied the Scalises' petition for a review of the case.

It was the BSA that did the suing in Broward County, Florida, where the school district had for years allowed many community groups to use school facilities after hours. After the U.S. Supreme Court's ruling in the Dale case, upholding the BSA's right under the First Amendment to set its own membership criteria, the Broward County School District sought to exclude the Scouts from using school facilities.

It cited a board nondiscrimination policy that applied to age, race, gender, religion, and sexual orientation. Other groups with distinct memberships—a youth orchestra, churches, a senior citizens' service, and an African-American sorority—were not excluded. In 2001, in *Boy Scouts of America vs. Till* (Frank Till was the superintendent of schools for the county), the BSA took the school district to court. The District Court ruled that the Broward County School Board had engaged in "viewpoint discrimination" against the Boy Scouts and granted a temporary injunction. The school board conceded, the injunction became permanent, and the school board paid the BSA's legal costs.

ACLU Threats

In their "war" on Christmas, the ACLU had often used the threat of a lawsuit to get a school district to cave in to its demand to remove references to Christmas in holiday programs or three-dimensional elements (e.g., creche scenes) from seasonal displays. The ACLU no doubt reasoned that nearly every public school district has a tight budget and few, if any, reserve funds so that defense of a lawsuit would cost it dearly. This, in turn, would lead many school boards to decide, "Why fight it?" and accede to the ACLU's demands.

They used this tactic in their first case under the new strategy, *Winkler vs. City of Chicago*, filed by Eugene Winkler and Kevin Poloncarz on April 10, 1997. The Roger Baldwin Foundation of the ACLU represented the plaintiffs. The suit was filed to force the city of Chicago to end its sponsorship of Boy Scout groups. A little more than nine months later, the city settled the suit, agreeing to the ACLU's demand. This success emboldened them to press on.

Less than four months later, the ACLU's Oregon regional affiliate represented an atheist mother, Nancy L. Powell, and her son, Remington, in *Powell vs. Bunn* ("*Powell I*"). Before this, Ms. Powell had complained to her son's school superintendent that the school was violating state law that prohibited support for religion when it permitted the Boy Scouts to use school facilities to recruit members. The superintendent turned down her complaint, so she sued in circuit court. Her suit sought review of the superintendent's decision as well as asserting that the Boy Scouts' use of the schools violated the Oregon state constitution's sections applying to religion. The circuit court rejected her claim and was upheld by the state's Court of Appeals. Finally, the Oregon Supreme Court on October 2, 2003, declined to review the case.

While this case was working its way through the appellate process, Ms. Powell brought a second suit on April 26, 2000, again *Powell vs. Bunn* ("*Powell II*"). The ACLU's Oregon arm again represented her. Her suit claimed that the school district discriminated against her son, also an atheist, on the basis of religion, in violation of state law. At issue, once again, was the fact that the school allowed the Boy Scouts the same access to its facilities as it did to similar groups.

The superintendent of schools again rejected her complaint. This time, however, the circuit court found that Ms. Powell had presented sufficient evidence of discrimination to cause it to send the case back to the superintendent to reconsider the matter. The school district appealed the decision to the Oregon Supreme Court, which concluded that the district's policy of allowing the Boy Scouts to give recruitment presentations on school property did not constitute discrimination under the state's law.

A handful of Muslim men regularly have the evening use of a room in the public library in Arcata on the north coast of California (*Reporter*, Eureka, CA, 1 October 2006). Their devotions are done in private and disturb no one. Perhaps this and other cases of Muslims using public facilities have never come to the attention of the ACLU. In any case, the ACLU's focus is almost exclusively on efforts to curb Christianity.

One must wonder, if the ACLU manages to kick the Scouts from schools after hours, what will stop them from kicking worship services out of schools on the weekend? Today in West Austin, almost every public school building leases space to a church for Sunday worship. This arrangement generates additional funding for the district, while providing start-up churches with a cheaper alternative to building their own facilities as they struggle to get on firm financial footing.

If they can stop after-hour Bible studies, or after-hour Scout meetings because of Scouting's adherence to a belief in God, why wouldn't they next set their sights on Sunday worship in schools, regardless of whether such organizations pay a fee for facilities?

Congress Acts

As the assault on the Boy Scouts grew more intense with both the ACLU's suits and those of others challenging Scouts' usage of public school facilities as violations of the First Amendment to the U.S. Constitution ("Congress shall make no law respecting establishment of religion . . ."), Congress acted. In 2001, after the Scalise suit was filed, members of Congress went to work to include in the No Child Left Behind Act the Boy Scouts of America Equal Access to Schools amendment.

Then-senator Jesse Helms of North Carolina was the lead sponsor in the Senate; Representative Van Hilleary of Tennessee was the lead sponsor in the House. Senator Helms minced no words when he introduced the amendment, saying, "School districts across America are now being pressured to kick the Boy Scouts of America out of federally-funded public school facilities . . . because the Boy Scouts will not agree to surrender their First Amendment rights and they will not accept the agenda of the radical left . . . . This arrogant discriminatory treatment of the Boy Scouts must not be allowed to continue."

The amendment passed in both houses and became a part of the No Child Left Behind Act, which in turn was signed by President George W. Bush on January 8, 2002. It specified that no school receiving U.S. Department of Education funds ". . . shall deny access or a fair opportunity to meet to, or discriminate against, any group officially affiliated with the Boy Scouts of America . . . that wishes to conduct a meeting within that designated open forum or limited public forum, including denying such access or opportunity or discriminating for reasons based on membership or leadership criteria or oath of allegiance to God and country of the Boy Scouts of America."

The Support Our Scouts Act was intended to protect Scouting's relationship with the federal government, including the ability to host the Jamboree on federal property. It also prohibits state or local governments that receive federal Community Development Block Grant funds from discriminating against Boy Scouts in government "forums" or from denying the Scouts access to facilities equal to those provided other groups. Under the act, if a state or local government fails to comply, the U.S. Department of Housing and Urban Development may terminate its CDBG funds.

This Congressional action had the effect of blunting lawsuits whose purpose was to deny the Scouts the use of public facilities. The ACLU and its allies were thwarted this time, but it soon became clear that, having been stung by the Dale decision, they intended to punish the Boy Scouts for not adhering to their definition of First Amendment rights.

The ACLU Shifts Strategy

They shifted their strategy away from schools. They have since pursued a two-pronged approach. One is to persuade municipalities and other civic entities to kick the Scouts out of facilities they have made available to them at nominal rents or rent-free. The other is to attempt to exclude the Scouts from participating in multi-charity drives, such as the United Way.

Efforts by the left to bring pressure on elected bodies, such as city councils, has had mixed results. One of these cases, *Evans vs. City of Berkeley*, did not involve the Boy Scouts' national organization directly, but was widely seen as part of the assault on Scouting. Since 1945, the city of Berkeley, California, had been granting free berthing space at the city marina to the Sea Scouts, an affiliate of the BSA. Other non-profit groups such as an association of disabled sailors and a women's sailing clinic also received free berthing space.

As do many cities, Berkeley has a nondiscrimination ordinance covering such things as age, sex, and disabilities. It also has one of the most liberal city councils in the nation. In early 1998, the city's Waterfront Commission reviewed the free marina berths for the Sea Scouts and other groups. Members of the commission expressed concern that the Boy Scouts of America's prohibition against active homosexuals and atheists was in conflict with the city's nondiscrimination ordinance.

The Sea Scouts, after conferring with the local council, the Mount Diablo Council of the BSA, wrote to the commission with this statement: "We actively recruit adult leaders and adolescents meeting the minimum age requirements without regard to sex, race, color, national origin, political affiliation, religious preference, marital status, physical handicap or medical condition. We believe that sexual orientation is a private matter, and we do not ask either adults or youths to divulge this information at any time."

The Waterfront Commission recommended that the City Council continue providing free berths to the Sea Scouts. The city manager, however, following the advice of the city attorney, concluded that the Sea Scouts were in violation of the city's nondiscrimination ordinance.

In early May 1998, the City Council voted to end the free berth policy for the Sea Scouts.

Believing that they were being singled out because the Boy Scouts of America denied membership to active gays and atheists, members of the Berkeley Sea Scout unit in 1999 sued the city. The lead plaintiff, Eugene Evans, was the volunteer adult leader of the group, and he was joined by thirteen other plaintiffs, including several youth members of the ethnically and economically diverse group. The suit claimed that Berkeley's denial of free berthing had, under the circumstances, violated the Sea Scouts' constitutional rights. The trial court denied the claim in June 2001.

In November 2002, the California Court of Appeals affirmed the lower court. Its position was that Berkeley had not denied the Sea Scouts their First Amendment rights, since the Sea Scouts remained free to continue their membership policies, and Berkeley was entitled to limit free berthing to those organizations that complied with the city's nondiscrimination policy. The state's Supreme Court upheld the lower courts.

Three regional affiliates of the ACLU filed *amicus curiae* briefs in support of Berkeley's defense of the case. They are the ACLU Foundation of Northern California, the ACLU Foundation of San Diego and Imperial Counties, and the ACLU Foundation of Southern California.

The Pacific Legal Foundation, a public interest law firm, handled the Sea Scouts case. Among those filing *amicus curiae* briefs in their support were the Pacific Justice Institute and the American Civil Rights Union.

The Jamboree Saved

For seventy years the Boy Scouts have had a Jamboree. It has become a tradition every four years for Scouts and their adult leaders from every state to gather on the red soil of the U.S. Army's Fort A. P. Hill in Virginia for a ten-day gathering of events, contests, meetings, and skill demonstrations. It is no small undertaking. The 2005 Jamboree drew some 40,000 participants and is estimated to have pumped $17 million into Virginia's economy.

Nevertheless, as part of its campaign to force the Boy Scouts of America to bend to its wishes as to membership criteria, the ACLU decided in 1999 to launch a lawsuit against the U.S. Department of Defense to bring to an end its sponsorship of Scout troops and its support for the Jamboree. Their lead plaintiff was Eugene Winkler, a member of the ACLU board of directors and former pastor of the First United Methodist Church in Chicago. This is the same Winkler who was the lead plaintiff in an ACLU suit against the City of Chicago's sponsorship of some Scout units.

This man of the cloth said, in conjunction with the suit, "Government neutrality in religious activities is a fundamental constitutional value embraced by most Americans. Government must be neutral because we are a nation of many religious views—as well as those who do not practice a religion. The expenditure of more than $29 million by the Pentagon for an organization that requires young people to believe in God . . . undermines this principle of neutrality" ("Prominent Chicago Religious Leaders Ask Federal Appellate Court to Protect Government Neutrality in Religion and End Extraordinary Funding for Boy Scout Jamboree," ACLU press release issued April 5, 2006 aclu.org/religion/govtfunding/24910prs20060405.html).

The suit targeted the DoD's logistical support of the quadrennial Jamboree, which was used by a number of Army reservists to fulfill their summer training requirement. It was also aimed at sponsorship by the DoD of BSA units overseas, and it challenged the distribution of any Community Block Grant funds to Scout units for use in programs aimed at helping economically disadvantaged youths.

In November 2004, the DoD entered into a settlement in which it agreed to remind military bases that official sponsorship of any nongovernment organization (such as the Boy Scouts) is prohibited. While ruling against the plaintiffs on other remaining issues, however, the district court held that military support of the Jamboree violated the First Amendment. On appeal, the Seventh Circuit Court reversed that ruling because the plaintiffs lacked "standing" to challenge the 1972 Jamboree Statute, which was the original authorization for government backing of the event.

The cost of providing logistical support for the Jamboree—in terms of personnel (largely reservists) and equipment—is approximately $7 million. Contrary to what the ACLU may want you to think, boys attending the Jamboree are not required to pray or to attend church at the gathering.

The next Jamboree is scheduled to skip a year from its quadrennial schedule. It will be held in 2010 to coincide with the centennial of the founding of the Boy Scouts of America.

The San Diego Case

Although the ACLU did not prevail in its effort to throw the Boy Scout Jamboree out of Fort A. P. Hill, chances are it will be back. The ACLU is nothing if not tenacious in its determination to have atheism (represented by approximately 5 percent of the population) prevail in the public square and to force the Boy Scouts to accept gay activists as scoutmasters and assistant scoutmasters.

The pressure continues in the case of *Barnes-Wallace vs. Boys Scouts of America* in San Diego. On August 28, 2000, a suit was filed by Lori and Lynn Barnes-Wallace, a lesbian couple, and their son Mitchell Barnes-Wallace, as well as Michael and Valerie Breen, an agnostic couple, and their son Maxwell, against the BSA and the city of San Diego. The suit was filed by the ACLU of San Diego and Imperial Counties exactly three months after the U.S. Supreme Court had ruled in favor of the Boy Scouts in the Dale case, thus upholding its First Amendment right as a private organization to determine its own criteria for membership.

At issue were two leases by the City of San Diego to the Desert Pacific Council of the BSA. One was for an 18-acre area of the city's Balboa Park and the other for a half-acre on Fiesta Island in Mission Bay, where the Scouts built (at a cost of $2 million) a Youth Aquatic Center. Under the terms of the leases, the Scouts pay only nominal rent, but are obligated to maintain both facilities for use by the public as well as the 12,000 Boy Scouts in the area. Also, other youth groups use both facilities extensively. In 2001 the city council voted to extend the Balboa lease for twenty-five years.

The Scout lease is one of approximately 100 leases of public land to non-profit groups by the city. Included in the list are the Girl Scouts, Salvation Army, a Jewish Community Center, and Presbyterian churches. Other groups receive cash subsidies from the city, though the Boy Scouts do not.

The adult plaintiffs said they refused to let their sons join the Boy Scouts because of its "duty to God" and "morally straight" membership requirements. As a result, they claimed, their sons lacked access to the campground. The Scouts countered with the argument that there is always extra space available for non-Scouts and that its facilities are used frequently by the public on a first-come, first-serve basis. They also noted that the city leases land to churches at nominal fees.

The Scout lawyer, George Davidson, made the point that the Scouts are not a religion. "There's no creed. There's no theology," he said. "It is an organization of people who come together on various principles, one of which is belief in God. But it's a very big tent. You can belong to any religion or no religion at all." ("High Court May Take Up Question of Scouts' Religious Status," San Francisco Chronicle, December 21, 2006)

Despite this argument, in July 2003 Federal District Judge Napoleon Jones ruled that the Scouts are a "religious organization with a religious purpose and faith-based mission." He said that the city, by giving the Scouts preferential treatment in the form of a no-bid lease, violated the constitutional separation of church and state.

On the basis of this ruling, the ACLU obtained a settlement that resulted in the City of San Diego canceling the Scouts' lease. It also collected for its own coffers $950,000 in legal fees and expenses—all paid for by the taxpayers.

The case was appealed to the Federal Ninth Circuit Court of Appeals. Of all the Circuit Courts of Appeals, the Ninth has had the most decisions overridden by the Supreme Court. Perhaps that is because it is widely seen as the nation's most liberal in its outlook. One need look no further than a decision by a Ninth Circuit panel to remove the phrase "under God" from the Pledge of Allegiance.

In the San Diego case, a three-judge panel of the Ninth heard the appeal in February 2006. In 2004, the U.S. Department of Justice filed an *amicus curiae* brief in the case, pointing out that requiring Scouts to profess belief in God does not make the BSA a religious organization any more than the requirement that Congress open its sessions with a prayer makes it a religious organization.

In December 2006, the panel voted 2 to 1 that the plaintiffs had "standing" to bring the suit, but put forward three questions to the California Supreme Court before deciding on the appeal. Subsequently, one of the panel's judges requested that the court review the case *en banc*, that is, with all justices hearing it together. That is where the matter stands as I write this book.

With Charity Toward Some and Malice Toward the Scouts

In 1999 the ACLU opened a new front in its war on the Boy Scouts. It sought to starve the Scouting movement of money by having it excluded from community charitable campaigns. Of the two cases in which it has been involved thus far, the ACLU has won one and the Boy Scouts of America the other.

The first, filed in November 1999, was *Boy Scouts of America vs. Wyman* (the Wyman in this case was Nancy Wyman, Comptroller of the State of Connecticut and a member of its Connecticut State Employee Campaign Committee). The Connecticut State Employee Campaign Committee had obtained a ruling from the Connecticut Commission on Human Rights and Opportunities to the effect that it was not required to include the Boy Scouts in its annual combined charities fund-raising campaign. Earlier, the ACLU's regional affiliate, the Connecticut Civil Liberties Union, had joined in a position statement urging such a ruling from the commission.

The BSA took the case to the Federal District Court. The BSA had participated in the campaign for thirty years, so it sought a ruling that it could continue for the year 2000 and into the future. The Scouts argued that they had a constitutional right to set their own criteria for members and therefore could exclude activist homosexuals. They pointed out that several other participants in the annual campaign had what amounted to discriminatory membership criteria. For example, the Girl Scouts obviously limited its membership to girls.

The National Black Child Development Institute was limited to African American children, and the Services for the Elderly of Farmington limited its services on the basis of age.

The defendants, the Connecticut State Employee Campaign Committee, acknowledged the Scouts' right to set its own membership criteria; however, it argued that to permit BSA participation, with its restriction on homosexual membership, would be to violate the state's Gay Rights Law. The court ruled in favor of the defendants.

The BSA then took the case to the Federal Second District Court of Appeals, which upheld the District Court decision. The U.S. Supreme Court declined to review the case.

The other case has had a more positive history for the Scouts. In July 2002, two years after the Supreme Court's ruling in the Dale case, Glenn Goodwin, an ACLU board member, brought suit in Federal District Court in the case of United States of America ex rel. *Glenn Goodwin vs. Old Baldy Council, Boy Scouts of America.* The ACLU Foundation of Southern California, a regional affiliate of the ACLU, represented the plaintiff throughout.

Goodwin's complaint alleged that the BSA's Old Baldy Council violated the federal False Claims Act when it accepted a $15,000 grant from the Community Development Block Grant program to provide economically disadvantaged youngsters an opportunity to participate in Scouting. Goodwin's complaint claimed that the BSA defrauded the government because its membership and leadership criteria are in conflict with the CDBG program's nondiscrimination requirements.

The BSA filed a motion for summary judgment, and it was granted by the District Court. The Ninth Circuit Court of Appeals affirmed the decision.

The Problem Continues

This will not stop the ACLU from its efforts to drive God from the public square or force the Boy Scouts to have activist gay scoutmasters. According to David Horowitz, president and founder of the Individual Rights Foundation, in a letter to supporters in June 2007, "At least 60 chapters of the United Way around the country have excluded the Boy Scouts of America from their funding."

In the same month the Philadelphia City Council became yet another public body to pull the plug on a special relationship between a municipal body and the BSA.

In an unexpected move, the council voted to end the 1928 lease "in perpetuity" the city had granted the Scouts for use of a landmark Beaux Arts-style building at nominal rent (a landmark that, by the way, the Boy Scouts had built). From this building the America's Cradle of Liberty Council of the BSA serves 64,000 boys in the Philadelphia metropolitan area.

Some city officials have expressed the hope that a compromise can be reached. If not, the Scouts are on one year's notice to vacate. Jeff Jubelirer, spokesman for the BSA Council, told the *Philadelphia Inquirer* (www.philly.com "Council Votes to End Lease With Boy Scouts," Philadelphia Inquirer, 1 June 2007) that "The real victims are the 40,000 kids of Philadelphia who potentially could lose after-school programs at a time when Philadelphia's murder rate is soaring."

The Crux of the Debate

The ACLU and like-minded liberals would have us believe that the Establishment Clause equates to freedom *from* religion rather than freedom *of* religion. Instead of a reasonable interpretation of the Constitution in a pluralistic society that protects our citizens from a state-sponsored religion being forced upon them, they want to take a more drastic step, which is to whitewash the public square and our public dialogue of any reference to God. Their view is that if one citizen believes there is no God, they must be protected from public references to or acknowledgment of an Almighty Creator.

In an effort to protect a minority view, they go so far as to maintain the position that an atheist, or a non-Christian, cannot be exposed to the majority religious viewpoints in America without unduly being indoctrinated. What about believing enough in your fellow men and women to acknowledge that maybe they can think for themselves? What about the educational value inherent in Christian children being exposed to a *menorah*, and Jewish children to a Christmas tree?

Recognition of the Almighty—even public reverence for Him—does not equate to indoctrination. And with something so pluralistic as the Boy Scout Oath, which doesn't mention attributes of God that would align to a specific faith viewpoint, a Muslim Scout can say it in keeping with his faith, just as a Christian Scout can with his.

So what are we to make of these attacks? I believe one way to see them is as a form of extremism that takes a seemingly virtuous position (i.e., tolerating minority views in keeping with a great American tradition) and transforms it into attempted domination of those who maintain a majority view. In other words, when they get their way, the ACLU enforces upon us the tyranny of the minority.

Let's be clear: I don't believe government, which taxes people regardless of their faith, should espouse a specific faith. I also don't think we should allow a small minority of atheists to sanitize our civil dialogue on religious references. They protesteth too much. It's as if the mere mention of a Creator is too powerful an idea for their own Godless ideology to withstand. Perhaps that's because there is a grain of truth to the idea that, indeed, all of Creation does speak to the existence of God.

Bringing it back to the Scouts for a moment, are we to teach them to be stewards of the great outdoors—to value our air, land, and water—and yet not say a word about the evidence that suggests this grand creation did not occur by chance? Are we to ignore that the universe is carefully and precisely crafted to sustain life, and that if gravitational force were slightly altered, the formation of the galaxy wouldn't have been possible? Science will never fully conclude that God exists, but does that mean that the weight of evidence offered by creation—the very creation we teach young Scouts to revere—does not point to an Intelligent Being as the most likely explanation?

Even if one goes along with the atheists' argument that life evolved from previous forms, where did the previous forms come from? They might say a more primitive form. Where, then, did that come from? Perhaps some primordial ooze. Where did that come from? From cosmic dust. And where did it come from? The Big Bang. Okay, who or what set off the Big Bang?

At some point they run out of answers and tell you they cannot explain where the essence of life comes from, and yet some refuse to ponder whether that source could be a self-existent Being that many of us call God.

In the context of science, are we not to encourage our children to follow the evidence? Are we to tell young Scouts, take care of the teeming life in this universe, but do not acknowledge nor ponder the existence of a life-giving force?

One of the most memorable Scouting events in my life, the National Jamboree in Valley Forge, Pennsylvania, in 1964, also brought me to our nation's capitol. In fact, I was the troop scribe, recording our events each day.

During our trip we visited grand monuments that stand in testimony to the wisdom and vision of our Founding Fathers, such as Washington and Jefferson, and the protector of the Republic, Lincoln.

Do we really think that, when our Constitution was adopted, Washington, Jefferson, and the other Founding Fathers intended to prevent any acknowledgment of the God they often credited with the birth of the Republic? The evidence says "No"—even for the Deist Jefferson. I wonder what Washington would say if he were in a courtroom today watching an ACLU attorney argue that our Constitution prevents the mention of the Almighty in a public setting. I think he might shake his head and say something along these lines: "We did not want King George to force his Anglican beliefs upon the colonists, but our war was not to protect children from the 'corrosive presence' of a Christmas tree."

Some intolerant things are done in the name of "tolerance." Christmas wreaths, displays of the Ten Commandments, and other religious symbols are torn down in the name of pluralistic tolerance, but such acts are in their own way a great display of intolerance. And for what? To prevent one child in a schoolroom from feeling "uncomfortable"?

There is a case in North Texas revolving around a class of students that sent cards to troops overseas wishing them well. One young man wanted to wish them "Merry Christmas." The school said he could not because it would violate the law. What are young children to make of the notion that the God they are taught to worship on Sunday has no place in their lives Monday through Friday while they sit in the classroom? What if we let the student who wants to express Christmas wishes do so, alongside the student who wants to issue greetings in the spirit of Chanukah?

The faith that permeates the lives of so many middle Americans is often derided as a crutch for weak people. This seems to be the view of many liberal elitists who worship the false idol of self. The views of a great many Americans are cast aside as over-simplified, and the liberal intelligentsia like to think of themselves as the only legitimate arbiters of morality. They think the public simply doesn't know better and is easily manipulated by the emotional appeals of troglodyte, conservative commentators. The people cannot have what they want, but instead should be told what they need. Liberal elitists have a low opinion of their fellow man and woman, hence the "need" to protect us from ourselves and our "irrational" passions.

Collateral Damage

The ACLU's "fingerprints" aren't on every effort to deny the Boy Scouts access to public facilities and events, though chances are they cheer when kindred groups initiate such efforts.

Take the case of the 2002 Winter Olympics in Salt Lake City. In the planning stages, when it was faltering financially, Mitt Romney stepped in as president and chief executive officer. He soon straightened things out and set plans in motion to make it a success.

In 2000 he put out a published call for volunteers: "Our state [Utah] has a strong volunteer heritage that has endured—the Olympic Spirit—for generations. The 2002 Olympic and Paralympic Winter Games will provide a chance for thousands of Utahans to participate through volunteering. And it is only through volunteer support that we can succeed in 2002." The summer of 2000 also saw a number of protests by gay activist groups around the country, following the U.S. Supreme Court's decision in the Dale case in June.

The Great Salt Lake Council of the BSA, the largest in the nation, with some 80,000 Scouts and 35,000 adult leaders, answered Romney's call for volunteers. For several months it had been meeting

As a part of our trip to the National Jamboree in Valley Forge in 1964, we visited Washington, D.C. Here we are with our local congressman, Omar Burleson, on the steps of our nation's capitol.

The Boys from Paint Creek. I wouldn't want to spend a Saturday with anyone but these fellow Scouts (I am in the front row, second from the left.)

Troop 48 practices first aid. These kinds of basic exercises by scouts have saved
many lives.

Merging my rural roots with a "take charge attitude" learned in Scouting. Here I
am driving the farm tractor – surely I must have had a hardship license by then –
proudly adorned in my scout uniform with a load of local kids in the back.

Here is our troop dog Tramp. This is a rare moment when he wasn't bandaged up from our first aid practice. Tramp was acquitted by a troop jury for eating our provisions.

Members of Troop 48 build a fire during a campout. My love for Texas A&M is already on display. We learned at an early age how to survive in the outdoors, and how to respect Mother Nature.

In my Cub Scout uniform, I display a rare smile in my sister Milla's presence.

Setting up tents for a Camporee.

Simulating a tent outline.

Finishing the line of tents.

Many Hollywood personalities visited the Irvine Ranch Jamboree in 1953, including Monte Montana and Debbie Reynolds (above).

Pioneer Scout leader "Uncle" Dan Beard is honored on Boy Scout Day, his 90th birthday, at the New York World's Fair, 1940.

Scouts detrain for the 1964 Jamboree I attended at Valley Forge, Pennsylvania.

Raising the flag at Jamboree headquarters, Valley Forge. Future Governor of Texas Rick Perry was there.

President Lyndon Johnson addresses the Valley Forge Jamboree, 1964.

Closing ceremonies at Valley Forge.

BSA Corps Seal: The symbol of millions of
Scouts and their famous motto.

Guidon leads Scouts to the opening ceremonies, Jamboree 2005 at Fort A.P. Hill, Virginia.

In 2005 Scouts still wait for the opening ceremonies to begin, as we did back in 1964.

Another Texas president attends a jamboree 40 years later with 40,000 Scouts on hand.

Presenting in the color at the closing ceremonies.

Balloons ready to ascend at the closing ceremonies.

Scouts learn the value of teamwork during feats of strength. In this case, the dreaded rope climb.

Scouting's utility applies to chores at home too!

Scouting teaches survival in the harshest conditions. Here, Scouts brave a snow-storm, equipped with snowshoes, packs, and the training they have received on a great many campouts.

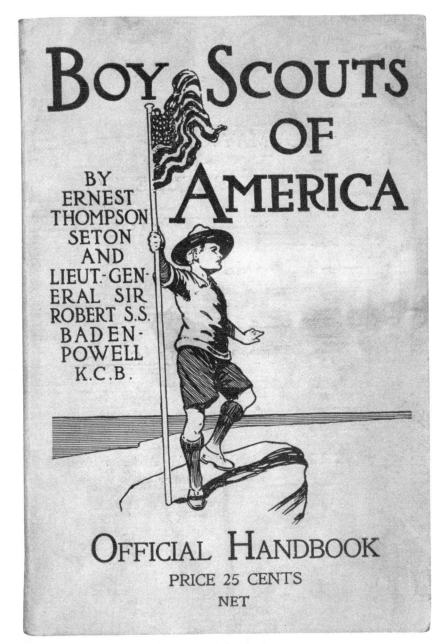

A copy of the first Boy Scout Manual, written by Scouting's founders. Thought to be an effective young way to prepare boys for the eventuality of military service, Scouting would blossom into so much more during the second half of the 20th Century.

The object of most every scout's desire and the symbol of youthful perseverance: the Eagle Award. Recipients of Scouting's highest honor, Eagles are an elite cadre of Scouting's best, and some of the nation's most successful private and public sector leaders have earned the Eagle Award.

Some of Scouting's earliest leaders.

Young Scouts learn practical skills, such as how to get a campfire going and how to cook out.

Whether it is canoeing or swimming, Scouts learn how to thrive in the water.

The admonition to "be prepared" includes having the right utensils to cook out. Likely, these Scouts also learned how to clean up their campout site before leaving, living up to the expectation that they would leave the land as they found it.

Scouting can be enjoyed by boys of all backgrounds and conditions, including those living with disabilities.

A portrait of Scouting's founder, Lord Baden-Powell. I was one of many Scouts who heard his widow speak at the National Jamboree in 1964.

Scouts doing their duty to God and country.

One of the most useful skills learned in Scouting is how to tie secure knots with ropes.

Early Scouts work as a team to haul cut-down trees – a scene not unfamiliar to Aggies who have built the campus bonfire.

The famous Fleur-de-Lis

Repelling: a valuable skill, especially for those who pursue a career in the military.

Troop 55 Scouts work to secure their troop gateway to their camping site.

Young Scouts enjoy the moment of a lifetime: meeting President Bush.

Determined young Scouts march off with packs, prepared for what the wilderness throws their way.

A Scout practiced in the art of building a fire gets his kindling ready.

A Cub Scout hike through nature led by adult Scout leaders.

The opportunities to learn respect for the outdoors and the animals that inhabit our planet are immense in the Scouts. Horseback riding helps develop a healthy respect for both.

Out of the Past: A portrait that spans the ages of Scouting in America.

Eagle Court of Honor: A striking portrait of the penultimate moment in a Scout's career: the Eagle Court of Honor ceremony.

Scouts bow in prayer to God. Though Scouting has not yielded on its recognition of God in the Scout Oath, it is nonetheless worth pointing out that Scouting's appeal to the Almighty is completely pluralistic, respectful of all faiths that acknowledge the Creator.

with Olympic officials under the assumption that the Scouts would participate as they had at the 1996 Atlanta Summer Olympics, working at many venues and participating in various ceremonies.

Sometime that fall, however, the Scouts were advised that they were no longer welcome to participate. Chief Scout executive for the council Marty Latimer said, "We don't understand what's wrong. They just don't want us and won't talk to us." He said that Romney had not returned calls from several Scout executives seeking an explanation.

The council's president, R. Lawry Hunsaker, expressed surprise that Romney had ignored Scout leaders, for he had once been a Scout and a Scout leader himself. "We can't get him to return our calls," Hunsaker said.

Plans had been underway to build a dormitory at the Scouts' Camp Tracy to house Olympic food service workers, but Olympic officials, without explanation, said they were no longer interested in doing this.

An Olympic spokeswoman, Caroline Shaw, denied that the Scouts had been shut out because of gay protests over the *Dale* decision. She gave a lame excuse, telling one reporter, "The reality is we would love to take those volunteers, but we have an age requirement for our volunteers. I believe it is 18." She added that Scouts and their adult leaders were welcome to apply as volunteers individually, but not as a group and, if they did volunteer, they could not wear their Scout uniforms (David M. Bresnahan, "2002 Bans Boy Scouts from Olympics," NewsMax.com, December 18, 2000, archvive.newsmax.com/archives/articles/2000/12/15/214301.shtml).

It turned out that there were youngsters under eighteen years of age participating in Olympic ceremonies, but these were dubbed by hair-splitting Olympic officials as "cast members."

Several years have gone by, and neither Mitt Romney nor anyone else who served as an official of the 2002 Winter Olympics has given a clear and logical explanation of why the door to volunteerism was shut on a willing "army" of Boy Scout volunteers. With the previous financial problems and bribery accusations associated with the Salt Lake Olympics before Romney came on board, it may be that organizers decided to forego the threat of a lawsuit by excluding Scout participation. In the absence of an explanation, it is difficult to avoid the conclusion that the decision was made as a reaction to the protests of gay activist groups to the Supreme Court's decision affirming Scouting's First Amendment rights. Whether pressure from gay rights groups caused Olympic organizers to resist volunteer assistance from the Scouts, we know that Romney, as a political candidate in the politically liberals state of Massachusetts, has parted ways with the Scouts on its policies over the involvement of gay individuals in Scout activities. He once said during a debate with Senator Ted Kennedy in 1994, "I feel that all people should be allowed to participate in the Boy Scouts regardless of their sexual orientation." ("On Boards, Silence On Gay Concerns," by Stephanie Ebbert and Benjamin Gedan, The Boston Globe, October 18, 2002, Friday, p. B1.)

The Liberals' Reach Extends to Government

If the liberal elites were only to try to chip away at the values of society from the outside, it might not matter except in the particular cases where their narrow view prevails. The fact is, however, they are entrenched in public positions of power, wielding the levers of control in public institutions across the country. One such notorious example is their influence over higher education and their unassailable position because of the protection offered by tenure. Academics have almost as much job security as federal judges; they are almost as hard to fire. Each year our colleges graduate young people with degrees in fields such as journalism and political science who have been taught that corporations are evil, religion is the opiate of the masses, and morality is relative.

This worldview took hold in the upheaval of the 1960s and 1970s, when all authority figures were questioned and self was elevated above the good of society. These values were in contrast to what the previous generation believed as it sacrificed to win a world war. Scouting—which instills the values of service to others, respect for authority, and character refined by hard work—mirrored the values taught by previous generations. Thus, when some worked to transform America into a society of the self-indulgent that craved free love and the quick fix of hallucinatory drugs, we saw battle lines begin to form between the proponents of extreme individualism and the traditional advocates of the notion that there are causes greater than self.

Each year liberal professors filled hundreds of thousands of young minds with lectures that would prepare them to enter the adult world with an outlook centered on self. Soon corporate America adjusted its advertising appeals, offering a barrage of messages aimed at self-gratification, such as an automobile maker that told us to "Look out for number 1." A common bumper sticker seemed to reflect this new attitude of self-indulgence, telling us, "He who dies with the most toys wins."

Where do such obvious appeals to self lead us? Clearly America is now the most prosperous nation in history. This is not a bad thing. Such a collection of resources allows us to do a great deal of good. Yet, we have one of the worst rates of crime in the wealthy Western world. We have a large number of people trapped by addiction and debt. Our great wealth has done little to end inner-city poverty or to improve our educational standing among the industrial nations. For all these problems, money is part of the answer, but money alone won't fill the human heart; it won't remove the stain of addiction, and it is a poor substitute for the absence of selfless values.

Scouting is more important than ever because our children are under assault by the culture, which bombards them with messages aimed at elevating self and materialism. They need a safe refuge that cultivates their minds with the values of service and sacrifice.

The liberals hold institutional power within the framework of many governmental institutions, too. In these chapters I have cited several cases where the Scouts went to court with human rights commissions. These commissions, formed for the ostensible purpose of protecting rights, are often nothing more than a front for attacking institutions that teach traditional values.

Officeholders are afraid to oppose the formation of an agency or commission whose title invokes a sense of justice (after all, who wants to be seen as being against human rights?). They turn a blind eye to the real purpose of such agencies, which often exist to enforce quotas and to challenge the values of most Americans in order to promote an agenda of individualism and license.

The agenda of the liberal inheritors of the counterculture mantle of the 1960s and 1970s seems to be to get their hands into every corner of government and education. They have been successful in many of our colleges and universities, from which the vast majority of our future leaders will emerge. They have infected the judiciary, where appointments often last a lifetime. They have become a part of the framework of government, where it is harder to kill an agency or commission than it is to defeat an elected officeholder.

When a human rights commission sues the Scouts, it may not win the battle, but it gains a little more ground in the war of attrition. That's because it takes resources for the Scouts to fight this war, and even victory can be costly.

The counterculture movement has also effectively positioned its non-profit organizations for receiving public resources and the private charitable donations of public employees.

While dozens of local chapters of the United Way have dropped the BSA from their lists of charitable causes, many liberal organizations receive approval for charitable donations as part of charity drives organized by the public sector. In Texas, the State Employees Charitable Campaign was created in 1993 as a means for state workers voluntarily to direct payroll deductions to health and human services agencies. Though one might think of non-political groups such as the Red Cross and Salvation Army as the intended recipients, groups such as the Texas Abortion and Reproductive Action League and the Austin-based liberal environment organization Save Our Springs were included as eligible recipients, despite their litigious history against the public sector and a prohibition against using charitable donations for litigation purposes ("Followup: State charities program still funding activism," *Lone Star Report*, 14 April 2000).

Armed with charitable funds, and often unable to enact their agenda at the ballot box or in the legislative arena, these groups turn to legislation by litigation. They seek from one judge what the electorate won't give them. That way their ideas do not have to have mass appeal. This is why the stakes are so high over the appointment of judges.

Judges can ignore the often silent majority and the ideas of the Founding Fathers, as they can base decisions on desired contemporary outcomes.

The Scouts are just one of many organizations under assault by such an approach. They are just one front in a multifaceted war. If, however, the counterculture activists can take down the Scouts, they will have gone a long way toward imposing a culture of self and moral relativism on the entire nation.

Individualism Run Amok

It is not my intent in this book to portray liberals as willing accomplices of the ACLU. There are people of all walks of life to whom Scouting appeals—liberals, independents, moderates—not just conservatives like me. There is a strong movement of people on the political left and center who love the outdoors and who support organizations that teach its stewardship. Many liberals despise the actions of the ACLU, not only because it may appear to distort their own politics, but also because they believe the ACLU's actions are damaging to America.

It is not also my intention to describe the ACLU agenda as representing a large movement in America. They are the perpetual "squeaky wheel that gets the grease." They complain so loudly and act so litigiously—often claiming to protect those who don't want their help—that one would think they represent a large force in American society. They do not. Their agenda is too extreme and their tactics so uncompromising that they do not represent a large social or political movement.

Why spend so much time castigating their actions then? The reason is that they are well funded and their actions have gone beyond the point of view of the small minority they represent on the political spectrum.

The ACLU's purpose—protecting individual liberties—is a prime example of a virtuous cause becoming subverted by an extreme interpretation. Their view of individual liberties is often so distorted that it comes at the expense of social obligation and community solutions to problems that plague neighborhoods. For example, their uncompromising advocacy on behalf of the homeless leads to policies conducive to the continuation of conditions that are adverse to those they supposedly represent.

When the city of Los Angeles, led by Antonio Villaraigosa, a mayor with ACLU roots, passed an ordinance prohibiting people from camping out on city streets and sidewalks throughout the day, the ACLU sued ("Homeless Sprawl," *U.S. News & World Report*, 18 December 2006).

Their allies on the Ninth Court of Appeals—a left-liberal court that struck down the ban on partial-birth abortion and "under God" in the Pledge of Allegiance—sided with the ACLU in its claim of a constitutional violation of the "cruel and unusual punishment" clause. (This is the court, by the way, that has had more decisions overturned than any other federal appeals court.) The majority opinion, authored by Judge Kim Wardlaw, reasoned that since there are not enough shelter beds available for all of Los Angeles' homeless and the six plaintiffs were "involuntarily homeless," the ordinance was unconstitutional (Jack Dunphy, "The Constitutional Right to Be a Bum," opinion/editorial, *National Review Online*, 18 April 2006).

Recognizing that some people suddenly find themselves homeless because of tragic, unanticipated circumstances, I would not say that all homeless people are voluntarily in their predicament. Many homeless have chosen their lifestyle—not as a conscious lifestyle choice made in prior years of sobriety but through a series of decisions that not only led to their homelessness, but also perpetuate it. They choose to drink, they choose to get high, they choose to engage in a life of crime, and often they choose to do it all on the streets instead of in shelters where there is strict enforcement of prohibitions on such behavior.

The cause of the homeless is a sympathetic one. They need help. But the help they need is not an ACLU propagating their conditions, and often their illegal behavior, but instead the specific help the city offered: to make some of their behavior more difficult to engage in. If you take a hard approach to blight, then you create a disincentive for continuing blight. New York City has proven this through its "broken windows" policy. By fixing broken windows, cleaning up graffiti, and cracking down on this kind of illegal behavior, they found a compounding effect where cleaned areas were less likely to be victimized in the future. Yet, where landlords or the city didn't care, and damaged property was left in its broken condition, criminals saw that as an invitation for continued illegal activity on the premise because, to them, there was an unspoken message that the owners and the city didn't care.

Far from criminalizing homelessness, the city of Los Angeles and its police chief William Bratton—the former New York City police commissioner who implemented the "broken windows" policy under the direction of former mayor Rudy Giuliani—were trying to clean up the conditions that invite further crime. Would their actions simply move the homeless to other parts of town? In some cases, yes, but there is something to be said for making illegal activity harder to perform on the grounds that it is at least an indirect incentive to find help.

The ACLU's actions do not help the homeless; they perpetuate their conditions. Supporters will say the public sector enforcers of such a policy are heartless, such as the city of Las Vegas, which sought to prevent feeding the homeless outside of sanctioned places intended for feeding them. The ACLU thought otherwise and acted accordingly. Is it merciful to allow people to continue in their misery? I don't think so.

In the Name of the Poor, but Not in Their Interest

Perhaps most tragic is the ACLU's legal insertion into new community policies initiated by the law-abiding poor to protect their homes and families from youth gangs and drug traffickers. The ACLU does the most damage when its lawyers show up and seek an injunction against night curfews and other crime-prevention techniques initiated by minority community leaders trying to make their communities safer.

The American Enterprise magazine in its July/August 1997 edition exposed the tragic consequences of ACLU legal action in Chicago. The Chicago Public Housing Authority began conducting random sweeps in public housing projects in search of drugs and guns. The sweeps were initiated by members of the community fed up with crime and were beginning to have a deterrent impact. Then the ACLU showed up. They filed suit, saying the sweeps violated the Fourth Amendment concerning unreasonable search and seizure. The result of the suit was to turn the Housing Authority's policy into a joke because it was forced to provide advance notice to gang leaders and their supporters before conducting a sweep, and tenants could forbid them from entering. Meanwhile, the rapes, the beatings, and the shootings go on, thanks to the ACLU and its crusade for the "rights" of criminal thugs.

Whether it is protecting the rights of pornographers, molesters, perverts, terrorists, garden-variety thugs, or those merely hostile to a belief in God, the ACLU is there to provide aid and comfort, in addition to a well-funded legal arsenal. They also fight reasonable local policies, such as school uniforms and, as I noted earlier, teen curfews. The ACLU fought the latter on the grounds that curfews might prevent teens from participating in late-night political events ("The ACLU blocks common sense and freedom," *The American Enterprise*, July/August 1997).

When a library discovered that the homeless were much more likely to fail to return books they had checked out, it implemented a policy restricting borrowing by people who lacked a permanent address. Enter the ACLU to say this was discriminatory. Before the matter went to trial, the library's board of directors backed down. Never mind that some homeless individual had been abusing the borrowing policies out of proportion to the general population ("Homeless patrons win in Worcester," *American Libraries*, October 2006).

Free Speech Zealotry

While the ACLU members may be litigious advocates of licentious behavior, you have to at least hand it to them that there is no argument they will not make, including the absurd. When the Internet Corporation for Assigned Names and Numbers (ICANN) proposed a ".xxx" domain name suffix for pornographic sites to help filtering software protect children from obscene content, ACLU representative

Marv Johnson said, "It's dangerous from a free speech aspect. How do you define what content is porn and what is just a Victoria's Secret ad?" ("Sex, lies and cyberpower," *New Scientist*, 3 September 2005).

Never mind that any site that ends with ".xxx" instead of ".com," ".net," ".edu" or ".org" can be automatically identified as pornographic both by filtering software and parents, the greater danger to the ACLU was the threat to free speech, even though no adult would be prohibited from viewing such material if they so chose.

In another case, the ACLU defended four neo-Nazis who wore lapel pins with a swastika into a German restaurant in California. The facts of this case, as chronicled by David Bernstein, the author of *You Can't Say That!*, demonstrate that the ACLU leapt to the defense of the neo-Nazis who filed suit after being refused service. Though one could argue that this shows the purity of the ACLU's thinking—that its members would argue on behalf of a group that they are philosophically aligned against—it had argued previously for "hate speech" regulations. So, the web the ACLU weaves has it twisted in some serious knots. Its members are for free speech, but not always when they disagree with the expression (such as when teens have worn shirts to school opposing the gay lifestyle).

Perhaps most stunning is how often they side against law-abiding people on behalf of criminals, predators, and thugs, even if ostensibly for some lofty reason or ideal. The New Jersey chapter of the ACLU sought to throw out state sanctions prohibiting ex-felons from voting, claiming they were being disenfranchised ("ACLU gets involved in debate for voting rights for ex-felons in New Jersey," *New York Amsterdam News*, 30 November 2006).

One of its allies in the fight, Rutgers professor Frank Askin, referred to such voting restrictions "as the last vestige of slavery." The ACLU argued in its suit that because the ex-felon population is disproportionately made up of racial minority members, the voting prohibitions were discriminatory.

While I think it is important for society at large to be sensitive to the notion that members of the minority community, even today, are more likely to be targeted for criminal activity, that doesn't mean those convicted of wrongdoing should be given a break. If voting is a privilege, what's wrong with tying it to behavior expected of all American citizens?

Taking Their Argument to the Extreme

In standing up for the civil liberties of individuals—especially those of a minority race or religion—the ACLU has committed no offense. Such a purpose is noble; however, when they draw a sharp line, always on the side of the individual's right without considering the wider social ramifications, they have crossed over an invisible line between right and wrong.

In the ACLU scheme of things, if one person is "offended" by a religious display, thousands must be deprived of it in order to suit the desires of that individual. If the pornography business wants to help ensure the anonymity of its consumers by fighting the ".xxx" Internet suffix, it will hide behind the ACLU's arguments for freedom of speech. Meanwhile, society may suffer the harm of families torn apart and crime perpetrated by individuals whose sexual addictions are satiated only by behaviors that become so extreme they are illegal.

If a student mentions her faith, however, in a graduation speech, suddenly the school has a right to turn off the microphone ("Valedictorian sues Nevada school for cutting off Christian speech," Associated Press, 14 July 2006).

Such examples show us that the First Amendment is really just a convenient tool to espouse something greater: the ACLU's ultra-left agenda. Otherwise, they would defend the conservative Christian and not just the atheist, the Marine accused of a war crime and not just the terrorist sitting in a cell in Guantanamo.

The ACLU seems to be most interested in "political correctness." In their view, individual "rights" always trump community- or society-wide standards. When these collide with broader standards, the ACLU goes full-force ahead on the side of license. In effect, they have all their marbles in the box of individualism and cannot recognize the social consequences of the destructive forces they often support.

If the ACLU's view is taken to its logical extreme—if the right of the individual is paramount—then what is to stop a child from "divorcing" his parents if he wants to? If little Johnny is tired of having the television turned off and going to bed at eight o'clock, doesn't he have a constitutional "right" to pursue his own destiny and govern himself as an individual endowed with the right to make his own decisions?

If society cannot impose upon the individual a sense of decency, how is it that even punishment for rape, burglary, and murder is constitutional under the ACLU view? How can society impose its "morality" on such an individual, who has the right to determine his own sense of right and wrong? Where does the madness end? Who is the ACLU protecting when it files a litany of suits on behalf of criminals, terrorists, and other thugs while filing suit *against* the Boy Scouts, public entities that allow Christmas displays, and mayors cracking down on lewdness?

Something called social obligation trumps self-indulgence. We should be able to expect the exercise of basic manners instead of public lewdness. There is an educational and historical component to religiously inspired public displays that doesn't amount to proselytizing. Yes, the rights of individuals are important. Our Creator endows us "with certain unalienable rights." Individuals, however, cannot live outside a social compact. Rules must guide society. Sometimes the rules must protect society at large at the expense of individual expression when that expression is deemed harmful to others and society at large.

That the Boy Scouts of America (or any other organization for that matter) would teach social values and reverence for a Creator does not put them at odds with our constitutional principles or the Bill of Rights. More than that, these values build a better society, where people are lifted up because they do not see self-satisfaction as the paramount pursuit; rather, it is the well-being of society as a whole.

There is undoubtedly a place for legal organizations that file suits on behalf of aggrieved minority groups. Often today, however, the ACLU doesn't even confer with the minority interests it supposedly advocates before taking legal action. Its members dictate what is best for those minorities, and then go home at night to live in safe neighborhoods that aren't terrorized by gangs and drug traffickers.

The ACLU seeks an alternative reality to the one here on earth. Thus, it often puts itself in the way of solving problems by those of us who have decided this life is the best we have and want to make it better for one and all.

Is Scouting Relevant Today?

Based on statistics related to Scouting participation, the quick answer is that Scouting is relevant today. More young men attain the rank of Eagle than ever before. Yet, the question is not so much about participation as it is about Scouting's impact. Can the values of Scouting, conceived nearly 100 years ago, make a difference?

The answer to that question begins with the audience: what kind of world are the children of America inheriting today, compared with those of half a century ago? The data is startling, if not depressing. The modern divorce rate is now estimated at about 50 percent. The number of families headed by single mothers is 10 million (U.S. Census Bureau, 2005). Drug addiction claims millions of lives, as does the high school dropout problem. And the number of youth incarcerated today is stunning. So, in terms of a ready-made audience for the values espoused by Scouting, there is no question that the need is great.

Need alone does not equate desire. Children starving for attention have many options competing for their attention, some wholesome and many not. For many young men, the message they are taught on the street, in school, on television—nearly everywhere they turn—is that to be a man they must be tough. There are variations on this theme, from the extreme cases of gangs encouraging prospective members to commit heinous crimes to prove their toughness, to boys who are told "don't cry" when they are upset—in other words, tough it out.

The latter example is not exclusively bad. Some kids need to be encouraged to have a stiff upper lip.

Over time, however, subtle messages that tell young boys always to mask their feelings can become an entrenched outlook that infects their relationships for the rest of their lives. Instead of being vulnerable with someone they can trust, they may become accustomed to acting out their feelings with negative results. The hyperactivity found in some boys as young as a few months old may, over time, become channeled into an emotional imbalance because they have hidden their feelings for so long, and the pressures and stresses they feel have no emotional outlet.

We wonder why men, on average, die a few years earlier than women. My non-scientific, non-clinical explanation is that stress and anxiety, concealed over a lifetime, may eat away at a man mentally, then physically, until his body can take no more.

Although fathers who carry around their own scars may be ill equipped to "diagnose" concealed anxiety in their sons, at least on some level they can relate to what their boys face as they grow closer to adulthood and the responsibilities that lie ahead. What, though, is the single mother to do, who is not emotionally wired the same way as her son, who cannot relate to the world as he sees it because the world she experienced growing up was fundamentally different? What are these 10 million mothers to do?

Some mothers—single or married—have an emotional "sixth sense" that is a gift for the children they raise. They know when to discipline a child and when to simply put their arms around him or her because they sense that the best thing they can do at that moment is to show love. For many mothers, though, raising young boys is a challenge beyond their capabilities. Nothing they have experienced has prepared them for what they face: two-year-olds who recklessly "fly" from atop the bed to the ground without a single fear for their safety; five-year-olds afflicted with "ants in the pants" that no teacher can seem to cure when they go to school; eight-year-olds who come home with bloody noses because a game of touch football became a Worldwide Wrestling Event in about five seconds; an eleven-year-old who suddenly becomes withdrawn because the young girl of his dreams doesn't know he exists; fourteen- and fifteen-year-olds who act up in school, stay out past curfew with friends who are a bad influence, or come home drunk, all the while wishing they could spend time with their fathers and have the love they so desperately crave from that missing figure in their lives.

For these single mothers, I can only imagine the feeling of hopelessness they must experience in the face of raging hormones so different from the ones they recall as an adolescent. Fortunately, for these mothers, there are constructive social organizations in which adult men can inspire and be mentors to such young men in ways they cannot.

Growing boys need role models. The sad fact is that every adult is a potential role model, including the athlete caught cheating using performance-enhancing drugs; the parent who sets the example of watching hours of brain-numbing television; and priests and other men of the cloth caught in sexual abuse scandals. We tend to report bad behavior on the 24-hour news channels while ignoring the good examples found all around us, heightening the reach of scandal in our lives. I believe this can create a sort of self-fulfilling prophecy in some young people who can no longer draw a distinction between fame and infamy.

Still, those positive role models are there, and not just in the Boy Scouts of America. There are good programs at the YMCA, Boys and Girls Clubs, houses of worship, and on the athletic field. For some young men, Boy Scouts may not be "the answer." But for many, it has been "an answer."

Some young boys—especially those with severe Attention Deficit Disorder (ADD), as I must have had as a boy—have never focused on something for more than a few minutes until they tried to build their first fire on a campout or learned to tie a bowline knot with a double half-hitch knot on the opposite end of a thirty-foot rope. Others have never been asked to do a project that takes more than a few hours or a few minutes to complete. If they have, they probably walked away from it without any consequences. Boy Scouts helps cure this form of restlessness. The combination of difficult tasks and harmless competition can ignite in a young boy the characteristic of perseverance that has never been seen in them before.

Former Secretary of Defense Donald Rumsfeld told me, "Scouting requires perseverance. When presented with the many distractions and activities—friends, sports, academics—there are many reasons to quit Scouting, but those who stick with it don't regret it. Certainly, I never have. I remember writing my father while he was aboard an aircraft carrier in the Pacific during WWII. I wrote that I was considering leaving the Boy Scouts. He wrote back and told me I could certainly do so, but he added: 'After all, quitting is easy. You quit one thing. Then you quit another. And, pretty soon, you're pretty good at quitting.' Needless to say, I stuck with Scouting—to my benefit."

If a single mother came to me and said, "How do I raise my boy to become a man?" I would tell her one way is to expose him to trustworthy adult male mentors, and there is no better place for that than the Boy Scouts of America. He will find role models he can look up to, and constructive engagement in specific tasks that will build his character, neither of which he is likely to find on MTV.

Furthermore, this mother will have an opportunity to bond with her son as part of Scouting, not only because Scouting now allows women to serve as adult leaders (a change in policy that was absolutely the right call), but because it gives mother and son something they can pursue together.

J. W. Marriott, Jr., told me, "As a Scout, I learned to appreciate my parents, especially my mother. She drove me to my troop meetings, and to my merit badge counselors, and she was always encouraging me to do more and to reach for the highest rank I could achieve. Without her encouragement and faith in me, I would have never earned the Eagle. I'm sure this is true of most Eagles and the reason why, when the Scout receives his Eagle, he gets to pin a small eagle on his mom."

Values to Live By

As discussed above, the Scout creed advocates twelve essential character traits. Scouts must be trustworthy, loyal, helpful, friendly, courteous, kind, obedient, cheerful, brave, clean, thrifty, and reverent.

Few people will quibble with these traits as goals, and yet it seems as if we have become used to expecting less in our actual relationships. Take the admonition to be kind and courteous. Those of us from Texas used to think rudeness was reserved for trips to New York City, where the people had a reputation for being confrontational and blunt. Yet, this is not only a gross generalization of New Yorkers, but to the extent that it is true about some of them, it is also true about the rest of society.

Yes, a good Southern gentleman will still open the door for a lady without expecting a women's lib activist to growl in his face about it, but you don't have to look far to find a culture so obsessed with self that we don't even think of the other person on the road, in line in front of us, or in the cubicle next to us. We Americans have developed poor manners.

I do not exclude myself from this indictment. In my case, acts of rudeness are shown on the television news all across Texas, as was the case when I was caught by a live microphone using vulgar language right after an interview with a Houston television reporter ended. I suppose that incident served to humanize me a bit, but only because such vulgar vernacular has become so common that people could identify with me showing a little frustration using "street talk." Nevertheless, it was wrong. It fell short of the standard I learned long ago in the Scouts: to be courteous and kind.

Similar words can be used to describe the American propensity for friendliness and cheerfulness. Society would say, again, "Nice ideals, but until I get my first cup of coffee and this kid in the back seat stops screaming at me, I am endowed with a God-given right to be down-right rude to anyone in my line of vision."

Neither cheerfulness nor friendliness are, in themselves, the gold standard. Plenty of people in politics, for instance, will stab you in the back with a smile on their faces. It only matters if it involves an inward transformation that manifests itself in the form of genuine, patient love. "Yes, I really would like to cut this conversation off with this person who won't stop talking, but maybe they just need someone to listen to them." In other words, I am not so important, and maybe the person could really use a friend right now. The common link in this inward exchange? Laying down one's own self-importance complex for the good of another.

Who wants to be around people who constantly bring others down? There is something to be said for an outward show of cheerfulness that, if practiced long enough, can become genuine if it wasn't real to begin with. It's a bit like this: you may be so tired you don't feel like reading *The Little Mermaid* to your three-year-old for the tenth time, but it amazes you that after you begin reading it, you actually sort of enjoy yourself, in part because the act of nurturing has its own rewards if we simply put "self" aside for another.

In discussing loyalty and obedience, we get down to brass tacks when it comes to the decline of modern society. Loyalty is in sharp decline. Take professional sports. The day "free agency" entered the equation in a major way, it signaled a virtual end to the idea of a superstar who played with the same team all of his career. Joe Dimaggio, Stan Musial, and Ted Williams gave way to the modern-day superstar—one even so great as Wayne Gretzky—one who would leave town and loyalty behind for more money or more celebrity in a larger market. I don't find total fault with this because there may be an issue of loyalty to one's family that can run crosscurrent to one's loyalty to team and town. Nowadays, however, there is also a sense that the teams and the players use one another for a shot at that one elusive "brass ring," knowing there is no long-term relationship in the cards.

Team owners are not exempt from this lack of loyalty. After the Marlins won the World Series in 1997, the owner engaged in a fire sale, leaving the franchise in shambles (though they managed to recover six years later and win again). It was as if he were saying, "I brought you the crown, so enjoy it for the off-season because we're taking this whole thing apart."

The message emanating often from pro sports franchises today is to win at all costs. The New England Patriots, not satisfied with Super Bowl victories and superior talent, were busted for illegally taping the New York Jets' defensive signals. The audacity of this move, when you consider that a Bill Belichick disciple coaches the Jets, is amazing. It is a classic case of "the ends justify the means." Winning, at all costs, including one's own integrity, matters most.

Obedience? I think the modern-day definition of obedience is doing what is right when the boss is watching. Our ethics have been reduced to outward appearance instead of inner strength. In hindsight, we know that the home runs flying out of ballparks in the late 1990s and the early part of this century were not real. Players averaging between thirty and forty home runs a year don't start breaking sixty homers several years in a row. Sure, they can get bigger arms in the weight room, but how does that explain larger necks? Unless the boss (the team owner), the commissioner, and to some extent the fans can prove a player used performance-enhancing substances, we engage in this fraudulent public debate in which we say we can't prove it, even though we know it. What do our children learn from this? They learn that the rules only apply when you are caught red-handed.

Obedience is doing what is right even if only God is watching. It reflects a form of character that is more than skin deep, and those that have it will be able to live their lives with consciences clear of the junk that comes from living a lie.

Obedience shouldn't be blind, of course. In that wonderful mini-series on HBO, *Band of Brothers*, the men had long assessed the gutless character of their superior officer, Lieutenant Dyke, before they got into a dangerous firefight with the Germans in the Battle of the Bulge. They knew they were sitting ducks as they stood behind an obstacle waiting for him to issue orders. Once he finally barked out orders, they also knew it wasn't based on a strong tactical assessment of the field of battle, but on fear, and that following those orders would have cost them their lives. Fortunately, they didn't have to make the choice of disobeying their superior officer because Captain Dyke was relieved of duty just in time, but had they disobeyed his commands, one could argue that disobedience was called for in this particular instance.

Most of the time, disobedience is a form of rebellion and a lack of respect for people in positions of authority. Reverence—another Scouting value—perhaps gets to the heart of our culture battle. Why would our youth respect their teachers, coaches, and bosses if they never were required to respect their parents? Reverence for authority starts in the home, where children learn the rewards and consequences of good behavior and bad.

I am not talking about reviving an era of stern discipline, such as the use of the belt or the switch. I am referring to parents who allow their children to develop a sense of self so at odds with society that those children cannot conceive of respecting their peers, let alone people in positions of authority. We would all gravitate toward monstrous behavior if no one socialized us. It seems to be our "wild" nature to do so, and only proper nurturing can redirect us. The one thing every child does have is an innate desire to please his parents, perhaps just in the hope of getting attention. This desire must be put to good use. Establishing boundaries and norms and requiring children to stick to those rules to receive approval is essential.

Recognizing that not every child is blessed with a good home, organizations such as the Boy Scouts can help fill the void, teaching good manners such as kindness and courteousness and instilling those deeper character traits, such as reverence, that can transform a young child's relationships for a lifetime.

The Scouting values of cleanliness and thriftiness also instill a form of respect: respect for one's surroundings and an economizing attitude toward use of those surroundings. Cleanliness in camping demonstrates a respect for the outdoors and for those who would subsequently enjoy such pristine places. Thriftiness discourages wastefulness in the accomplishment of a task, which is another form of respect both for the environment and those who would enjoy the same space.

The twelve Scouting values are not equal in importance in my mind, but each has its significance. The admonition to be clean does not carry the same weight as those to be brave or reverent, but it has its place because it carries over positively outside Scouting. When you consider the early ties between Scouting and the military, you can understand how cleanliness made it into the vaunted twelve. Military units have been lost because of carelessness in putting out a fire or cleaning up rations, thus leading the enemy to their trail.

Essential to the Scouting approach is the admonition to be helpful. This trait not only teaches young men about selflessness, but a sense of teamwork. The over-used expression "there is no 'I' in team" comes to mind. Teaching young men that there are "causes greater than self," as Senator McCain is fond of saying (with great credibility on the subject), is essential if we are to reclaim society from narcissism. If you teach a young man to help a fellow Scout out of the goodness of his heart, maybe you plant a seed that will sprout later in life in the form of a young man who volunteers as a Big Brother, a community leader who runs for office to solve others' problems, a CEO who is motivated by much more than the money he can make.

The call for bravery is an encouragement for young men to overcome their fears. Scouting doesn't reward failure with badges, but it also doesn't condemn failure. Young boys can only overcome their fear of failure—and that voice in their heads that says "you can't"—if they are first allowed to fail. Bravery does not always equal success, but it is the key ingredient in pursuing it.

I believe nothing worth earning in life comes easy. It is in facing our fears and overcoming our doubts that our character is refined like silver in the fire. The road to Eagle is arduous. It asks much of a young man, including surviving doubt. One could say that the process of overcoming fear is the same process as developing faith. Fear and faith are 180 degrees apart on the circle of attitude. It is not possible for us to have faith when we are absorbed by fear. And total faith crowds out fear.

Trust: The Key Trait

Trustworthiness is the apex of the Scouting values. I believe trust and faith are synonymous. Let me share a story to illustrate my point.

A tightrope walker had managed to a tie a rope to trees on both sides of Niagara Falls, and he proceeded to walk across the falls on the wire, and back, without falling to his death. A small crowd watched in amazement as he returned to safety.

He looked at the crowd and said, "Do you think I could push a wheelbarrow across this very same tightrope?" They were quiet, for fear of encouraging a form of stupidity that could lead to death. So away he went, walking the tightrope, pushing his wheelbarrow to the far side and back. They were amazed.

He decided to go further: "Do you think I could push a load of bricks in this wheelbarrow across the falls?" A few had become believers, and quietly nodded in ascent. Others were still afraid of the colossal fall about to happen. But he amazed them further with his deft agility as he safely went across and back.

By then, a large crowd had gathered. They were rapt with amazement. He emptied the bricks, looked at the astonished crowd, and said, "Do you think I could push a human being across the falls in this wheelbarrow?" By then they were all believers. All together, they shouted in affirmation.

Then he looked at them and said, "Who will be the first to get in?"

The idea of faith in America has been reduced to the concept of belief instead of elevated to the notion of trust. It is one thing to acknowledge or believe something as true. You can even have an emotional moment of affirmation when the truth grabs your heart, but it is quite another thing to give your life in trust to a cause, or in the most important sense, to God. In other words, a lot of people "believe in God," but few people actually get in the wheelbarrow and trust Him with their lives. Faith is not belief; it is trust. It is the turning over of all our priorities in the deepest sense of the soul to a Higher Being, knowing we will be better for it even if logic cannot conceive of this being true.

A lot of people in churches today believe in God but don't have faith in Him. Many churches reduce faith to outward acts instead of an inward transformation. Yet, going to church doesn't make someone a Christian any more than going to Yankee Stadium makes one a professional ballplayer. There's a reason Jesus said "narrow is the way" that leads to salvation.

Scouting espouses trust as the highest standard. Our fellow men ought to be able to trust us with their lives, knowing our character is of such a magnitude, proven by baptism of fire, that they would not doubt for a minute our propensity to do the right thing. Trusting man is an inexact science. The best of us make mistakes and break trust. It is in some ways simpler with God, even though He is unseen, because He will never fail us. Yet, if we give it our best over the long run, the many acts of decency, love, and sacrifice will outweigh the occasional moments of selfishness and sinfulness, meaning that people who are a part of our lives will be able to discern whether or not we are truly trustworthy.

When someone asks the question, "Can I trust you?" they are asking whether you are honest, whether you are dependable, whether your actions are as good as your word. Scouting is about raising young men whose actions live up to their words.

Much More

The benefits of Scouting extend beyond the character traits contained in the creed. As former senator Sam Nunn once put it, "Scouts learn survival skills in the wilderness, but also survival skills for daily life in modern America: resourcefulness, cooperation, leadership, and self-esteem."

Leadership is sorely missing in our society today. I speak not just of public figures in elected office who have let us down, but the lack of leadership in our neighborhoods and communities. Do teachers' unions care more about the education of children or the financial benefits of their membership? Do education administrators care more about the college graduation rate of their high school seniors or the size of their budgets and the number of slush funds at their disposal? Do pastors and priests care more about the number of attendees at services or the number of people who have been transformed by a renewed sense of faith? Do corporations care more about the profit they have turned or the investment they have made in their employees and their stewardship of community resources?

The old axiom is that no great civilization was conquered by a foreign power, but collapsed from within. It seems that the lessons learned by previous generations that build a great society get lost when times are better, the economy is stronger, and self-discipline has deteriorated. Those who fought in World War II are often called "the greatest generation" because of the sacrifice they made for freedom. They had just come out of the Great Depression. Thus, few were distracted by materialism and creature comforts. They had a greater sense of community. They knew the importance of sacrifice. And sacrifice they did.

But imagine if CNN had been present at Omaha Beach where thousands were slaughtered by German gunfire. Would we be able to overcome such tragedy today, or even recognize it as victory? To what extent would the Nazi regime have exploited American media reports about allied soldier abuses, as Al Qaeda and its allies do today? Would we, as a nation, be able to make the sacrifice that was required then?

Many individuals would do so today, in Afghanistan, Iraq, and in dangerous places all across the globe. Will we, though, have the leadership able to withstand public pressure and the defeatism of some to sustain causes involving our vital interests, no matter how high the cost?

Scouting teaches boys to stick to a task no matter how difficult or how long it takes. It takes years to earn an Eagle, and many more to advance through all the ranks of Scouting. The appeal of Scouting is not the quick thrill but the satisfaction of overcoming difficult obstacles. In a time of turmoil, don't we need more of that?

Scouting Heroes: Values in Action

When Matthew Mills jumped into the pool to save his twenty-month-old cousin, Ian, he acted so quickly that the adults sitting poolside didn't know what was happening until the toddler's head had emerged from the water. It was a near-tragedy that is all too commonplace at homes with pools, but the rescue was made all the more heroic because the eleven-year-old Boy Scout who saved Ian's life was born with a skeletal impairment that confined him to a wheelchair.

Matthew said of his heroic actions, "All I was thinking about was saving him, getting his head above water . . . I wasn't thinking about me at all" ("11-year-old Scout is something special—in many ways," *The Virginian-Pilot,* 21 November 2004).

Such is the Scouting way: thinking of others first. Matthew Mills is not the only extraordinary Scouting Good Samaritan, just one of the more compelling ones. Time and again young Scouts have come to the rescue, almost always in a calm, thoughtful manner because of their training. Most, like Matthew, when recognized with a Scouting honor medal, demur, saying they are not heroes or that they only wanted to help.

Twelve-year-old Michael McAnelly was at the beach with a group of boys and their fathers from the Church of Jesus Christ of Latter-day Saints. He heard his younger brother's voice in a panicked pitch and, in running in the direction of his voice, discovered that the boy's play-mate was immersed in the sand with only one leg sticking out. Acting quickly, he dug his feet in, placed the young boy's leg on his shoulder, and leaned forward like an ox, pulling with as much leverage as he could until the young boy came out, coughing and out of breath The *Contra Costa Times* reported ("Boy Scout a hero for saving friend," 9 February 2006): "In the end, Michael didn't see what he did as any great feat, considering that he has been a Boy Scout for about six years and is the son of a Boy Scout professional. He just did what he had been taught, he said. 'I've learned to not panic, and to try and be the first to do something about it,' Michael said."

The calmness of young Scouts in a crisis situation is striking, especially when compared to the panic that ensues among adults who may witness the same events. When Matthew Whalen, age thirteen, saw his aunt go into a seizure in the presence of a large number of family members, he took charge while the adults were confounded about what to do.

He commanded one family member to call 911 and told another to take the young girls out of the room. He then cleared his unconscious aunt's passageway and performed CPR.

Matthew told a reporter with the *Times Union* in Albany, New York ("Scout saves a woman's life," 29 November 2005), "I recognized the symptoms, and I did what they told me to do in Boy Scouts."

Eighteen-year-old William Berkey, an Eagle Scout, displayed such a "take-charge" attitude during a school rafting and camping trip. An oak tree at least fifty feet tall had fallen on sleeping students, trapping Ale Braga. Berkey gathered the students around the tree and positioned them to begin a lift.

When the tree was lifted, Berkey recognized that Braga was going into shock from a laceration to her thigh and the trauma of the event. Trying to keep her conscious, he folded her arms and had students hold her legs together, talking to her until rescue workers arrived. He then helped the rescue team carry her to the ambulance and rode in the ambulance with her to the hospital. One doctor credited Berkey with saving Braga's life. ("Ale Braga: Young Golfer Gets Back Into the Swing," San Francisco Chronicle, 18 July 2004)

In Bowling Green, Kentucky, in 2002, Matt Knight, a high school sophomore and a Boy Scout, rescued eighth grader Susan Beth Meeks from a drainage pipe full of water. He was practicing with his cross-country team when he heard her screams. She had fallen into the pipe at the end of a drainage ditch, lodging her foot under a rock in such a way that her head was in the water. Matt rushed into the pipe and pushed her out.

Matt told the Associated Press, "You know when you run sometimes and the last 100 meters feels like forever? That's how it felt." For his quick thinking and heroic act, Matt received Scouting's Honor Medal with Crossed Palms, one of only 167 recipients of it since it was created in 1930. ("Boy Scout to Meet President After Heroic Act," Associated Press, February 7, 2003.)

The Scouting program has an impact on young men in two ways significant to crisis situations: (1) it gives them practical first aid training so they are prepared to handle a variety of situations and think quickly on their feet; 2) it instills an ethic that they are always to help a neighbor in need.

When others resort to panic, Scouts often fall back on their training. Sometimes even the youngest Scouts show great courage. Gage Phillips, eight, was playing with his two-year-old brother when the toddler put a penny in his mouth and began to gag. Gage recognized little Noeh de la Rosa was choking and proceeded to save him.

Daily Oklahoman columnist Carrie Coppernoll detailed the incident: "'He choked on a penny and I gave him the Heimlich,' Gage said. The second-grader paused. His mom, Jeanna de la Rosa, encouraged him: 'Then what happened?'

"'He hurled on me.'" ("Cub Scout, 8, Comes to Rescue of Little Brother," Daily Oklahoman, 20 September 2006.)

Scouting's motto, "Be Prepared," emphasizes the importance of anticipating any crisis and being ready to handle it. With Scouting's origins tied to a military function, it also emphasizes the role Scouts have played from time to time in defending a nation at war.

British Prime Minister Winston Churchill gave a glowing tribute to the Scout movement spawned in Britain:

The success of the Scout movement led to its imitation in many countries, notably in Germany. There, too, the little troops began to march along the roads already trampled by the legions. The Great War swept across the world. Boy Scouts played their part. Their keen eyes were added to the watchers along the coasts; and in the air raids we saw the spectacle of children of twelve and fourteen performing with perfect coolness and composure the useful functions assigned to them in the streets and public offices. Many venerable, famous institutions and systems long honored by men perished in the storm; but the Boy Scout Movement survived. It survived not only the War, but the numbing reactions of the aftermath. While so many elements in the life and spirit of the victorious nations seemed to be lost in stupor, it flourished and grew increasingly. Its motto gathers new national significance as the years unfold upon our island. It speaks to every heart its message of duty and honor: "Be Prepared" to stand up faithfully for Right and Truth, however the winds may blow. (Winston S. Churchill, Great Contemporaries (Chicago: University of Chicago Press, 1973), p. 347.)

The Scout influence on members of the military, and cadets aspiring for military service, is profound. Reading the obituaries of soldiers who have died in Iraq and Afghanistan, it is astonishing to see how many were Scouts. The value of service taught in troop meetings becomes a way of life when they enlist, or become officers, in the United States military.

Scouting also prepares future soldiers, sailors, marines, and airmen for life in the field by imparting survival skills: a vital component of the intense training for SEALs and Army Rangers.

One young man training to be an officer in the military found his Scout training essential far from the field of battle. Midshipman 4th Class Roarke Baldwin, a freshman at the Naval Academy, received the Navy Achievement Medal for running toward gunfire at the Westfield Annapolis Mall and rendering aid to an off-duty Secret Service agent who had intervened in a dispute. The agent, shot in the thigh, fired six shots at his assailants from the ground. When Baldwin arrived on the scene, he provided aid to the agent by putting pressure on the wound. He subsequently assisted the agent's wife and their eleven- and four-year-old daughters after the agent was airlifted to Baltimore ("Mid will get medal for helping shot agent," *Annapolis Capital,* Annapolis, MD, 17 January 2007).

"I wasn't thinking about being a hero, I just did what I knew to do," Baldwin told the *Annapolis Capital.*

Some of the stories of Scout heroism are almost unimaginable. By the age of fourteen, Anthony Marzocca had played a critical role in rescue operations twice. The account from *The Record* of Bergen County, New Jersey, is compelling:

On Dec. 28, 2003, Marzocca and his father, Paul and a friend of his and his sister, Charlotte, were driving on the Garden State Parkway when they saw a car in front of them veer off the road and hit a tree.

"It spun 180 degrees in the air, the engine exploded and caught fire," Marzocca said.

Marzocca and his father ran to the car and saw a girl, 8, and boy, 10, in the back seat crying. Their father, who had been driving, was slumped over on the passenger side of the front seat on top of his wife.

"You could only see her face," Marzocca said.

Marzocca and his father tried to pull the doors open but they were locked. Marzocca ran to another motorist who had also stopped and asked if he had a fire extinguisher. The man told him, "No, but I have tools."

So Marzocca grabbed a screwdriver.

"I thought if I could break the door window I could get in but I couldn't," he remembered. " I went around to the back and saw the rear window had been blown out."

Marzocca climbed over the trunk (where the gas tank was) and saw the girl slumped over and her seat belt twisted. He unlocked the door on the boy's side, freed the girl and slid her out of the left rear door.

"There was blood coming down her left forehead," he recalled.

Then he got the boy out. Both parents, who Marzocca learned were on their way to open Christmas gifts, perished in the crash.

"It was a true feeling of helplessness," Marzocca said. "The doors were locked and you couldn't open the windows. You never think you will be put in that situation because you don't want anyone to be in that situation."

The rescue won Marzocca the Honor Medal from the Boy Scouts of America National Court of Honor.

Marzocca defined his heroic nature the moment he put aside the danger to his own life to save total strangers, but the rush to the rescue—regardless of the threat—had already shown itself when he was just 12 and helped save an injured skier who had skied off a cliff.

He was on a school trip at Mountain Creek in Vernon when, from a chair lift, he noticed a large group of people gathered below at the base of a trail.

He skied down from the top to people gathered at a drop because "it looked like there were people who might need help."

"A girl had missed a turn and hit a tree," he said. Marzocca skied down to her with another student.

"She had broken her leg where you could bleed out fast," he said. "We contained her leg and stabilized her. We put her on a backboard, then a sled and brought her up to an ambulance."

His actions won Marzocca the Heroism Award from the Boy Scouts of America National Court of Honor.

Marzocca's rush to help both times was spontaneous.

"I had to act," he said. "It needed to be done. There was no way I could sit there and not do anything." ("I had to act," 15 June 2006)

Perhaps Anthony was as influenced by his parents and his upbringing as he was by his Scouting experience during these crucial moments. Maybe a young man with no experience in the Scouts would have done the same thing at the scene of a tragic car accident (though it is doubtful he would have the same confidence in stabilizing a badly injured skier). It is not as if Scouting has a patent on virtue; however, it does offer a strong formula for it. And it gives young men the preparation needed to handle a variety of difficult situations.

Such Scouting heroism spans the generations. In August 1943 Jerry Clucas was a twelve-year-old boy playing on the edge of a canal in Idaho. Someone spotted a "doll" in the swift waters, and Clucas, seeing a diaper on it, realized it wasn't a doll but a baby.

Clucas dove into the water and grabbed the infant. Noticing it was swollen and blue, he carried it to a nearby barrel and gave it mouth-to-mouth recusitation, drawing on his training as a Sea Scout.

Clucas told the Associated Press, "I didn't do it right. But he lived .... I blew hard into his lungs. I can still see his little chest going up" ("Men reunite in Las Vegas, 61 years after river rescue," 13 March 2005).

Sixty-one years later, the fifteen-month-old baby Clucas saved—Dick Wood—was reacquainted with his hero through some inquiries initiated by Clucas upon meeting a couple from Idaho. Wood traveled to Las Vegas and shared his life story, including his tour of duty as a combat pilot in Vietnam. Hearing about Wood's service, Clucas decided he had learned what good had come from his act that day.

From a young boy using the "stop, drop, and roll" technique to save his flame-covered little brother from burning to death, to a thirteen-year-old Scout who saved his grandfather when their boat turned over in complete darkness, to a little Tiger Cub scout who pulled his mother's submerged head out of water when she had an accident and was knocked unconscious leaning over the bathtub, Scouts have responded to dire circumstances with life-saving heroics ("Big Brother, Big Hero," *Wisconsin State Journal*, 16 June 2005; "Boy Scout recognized for lifesaving act," *Minneapolis Star-Tribune*, 13 July 2005; "Fort Wainwright boy receives heroism award," The Associated Press, 2 October 2006).

More than 100 Scouts, of more than 900,000 nationwide in 2005, received the Heroism Award ("Scouts honored for heroics," *Oregon Mail Tribune*, 13 March 2006). For every act of heroism honored with a medal, there are countless other "good turns" done by Scouts not seeking glory or self-aggrandizement, but to do what they have been taught.

The test of character and courage sometimes occurs in the worst of circumstances, and later is magnified in the public eye. Most of the time, however, good character and small acts of courage go unnoticed by all but except a small few. Yet, those small acts, performed day after day, year after year, make for a monument of good will that serves as a tribute to this great program. If only every young man, whether through Scouting or some other constructive source, would have their character so shaped.

Scouting in a Changing World

Having failed in the courts to bend Scouting to their will, the ACLU and its allies have turned, as we have seen, to efforts to starve the Scouts of funding and access to public facilities. Their strategy has not achieved that goal. Nevertheless, it has cost the Scouts several million dollars to defend legal assaults and more than 100 years of litigation (the total years of cases measured from start to finish), according to David Park, national general counsel of the Boy Scouts of America. The Curran case, for example, stretched out over seventeen years.

The ACLU has been avid in its pursuit of city and county governments that decades ago accepted and placed in public buildings and parks plaques from a fraternal order listing the Ten Commandments. Their claim is that displaying the Commandments in public places constitutes government sponsorship of religion, although the Commandments are a code of good behavior. This campaign has had mixed results. In some cases, courts have required that the Commandments be removed, while in other cases they have allowed them to stay.

The culture war regularly plays out on new fronts. Recently in Oakland, California, a group of African American Christian women who are city government employees formed the Good News Employee Association (GNEA). They announced its formation with a flier defining their group as a "forum for people of Faith to express their views on the . . . issues of the day. With respect for the Natural Family, Marriage and Family Values."

They posted their flier on an employee bulletin board after various other employee groups had used the bulletin board and the city's e-mail system to advertise "gay rights" and various political views. They asked for formal approval to use the city's employee e-mail system and bulletin board regularly, but were denied on the grounds that their flier would "promote harassment based on sexual orientation."

Gay rights advocates employed by the city had used the communication system to promote "Happy Coming Out Day," but the city's bureaucratic overseers deemed the words "marriage" and "family values" unacceptable. Perhaps this was simply retaliation because of the conservative Right's use of the phrase "family values" and their efforts to prevent public recognition of gay marriage. But nonetheless, it should not be forgotten that, regardless of their distaste for middle America's views on the sanctity of marriage and its definition of family values, they declared too controversial a couple of the most wholesome notions in American society today.

This is but one example of efforts to limit free speech and to curb values that have been central to the American experience for many decades.

The ACLU and "Family Values"

The city of Oakland's unwillingness to allow employees to use the terms "family values" and "marriage" is matched by the ACLU's rousing defense of predatory pornographers of the National Association of Man-Boy Love of America (NAMBLA). This is in contrast to its apparent view that the Supreme Court's affirmation of Scouting's First Amendment rights was wrong and needed to be circumvented.

The ACLU sees itself as an arbiter of moral and legal behavior, yet it took up the cause of men who prey on boys when it defended the North American Man-Boy Love Association (NAMBLA) in a $200 million civil suit brought by Mr. and Mrs. Robert Curley of Cambridge, Massachusetts.

The Curleys' charge was that one Charles Jaynes was driven to sexual action by the Web site and literature of NAMBLA—an organization that promotes sex between men and boys as young as eight.

Jaynes and Salvatore Sicari actively sought a boy for their sexual pleasure. They picked ten-year-old Jeffrey Curley, who was playing outside his home in October 1997. They lured him into their car. That day, Jaynes had visited the NAMBLA Web site. Later, when Jeffrey resisted their efforts at molestation, they choked him with a gasoline-soaked rag until he was dead. Next, they took the body to Jaynes's apartment in Manchester, New Hampshire, where they molested it. Afterward they stuffed the boy's body into a container, filled it with cement, and dropped it in a river. It was recovered a few days later.

Jaynes and his accomplice were apprehended. The police investigation turned up NAMBLA literature in Jaynes's apartment. The men were tried, convicted, and are today serving life sentences in prison.

NAMBLA's now defunct Web site encourages men to get access to young boys by volunteering, for example, to work for the Boy Scouts. That's not all. Larry Frisoli, the Curleys' attorney, said NAMBLA publications are "actively training its members how to rape children and get away with it. They distribute child pornography and trade live children among NAMBLA members with the purpose of having sex with them."

Frisoli describes NAMBLA's "The Survival Manual: The Man's Guide to Staying Alive in Man-Boy Relationships" as telling members "how to gain the confidence of children's parents. Where to go to have sex with children so as not to get caught . . . [and] if one is caught, when to leave America and how to rip off credit card companies to get cash to finance your flight" (Deroy Murdock, "No Boy Scouts," *National Review Online*, February 27, 2004.).

In his diary, Jaynes expressed reservations about having sex with children until he discovered NAMBLA. This occurred about one year before he killed Jeffrey Curley.

The Curleys' case against NAMBLA as an organization was dismissed because it is not a corporation. The Curleys had the option to sue individual members.

The great irony here is that the ACLU chose to defend a depraved group whose purpose is to encourage men to molest boys. Meanwhile, it fights the Boy Scouts of America, whose purpose is to have men guide boys toward manhood through activities that promote health, teamwork, leadership, and character-building.

Values of Americans

To the ACLU, free speech by a group that promotes depraved conduct trumps community values. It has its supporters. Actions such as the defense of NAMBLA suggest that we Americans are at war with ourselves. The institutions we saw as bulwarks of stability—such as the Scouts—are under steady attack by groups that seem intent upon remaking (if not replacing) them in pursuit of a very different view of things.

Are there still community values? Do we Americans share some widely held ideas in common? In 2005 the Youth and Family Research Center of the Boy Scouts of America asked Harris Interactive, a major national polling firm, to find answers to these questions. It published its findings in a report entitled "Values of Americans: A Study of Ethics and Character." (scouting.org/media/research/02-849.pdf)

In the introduction to its study, Harris says, "American values and ethics are believed to be in a state of flux. Today, Americans face a bewildering range of lifestyle options, with complex and unprecedented decisions to make. With corporate ethics being questioned and the media reporting unethical acts by individuals in corporations and various organizations, Congress and lobbying, one wonders what values are important to Americans today. Do they still hold the ethics and values they held 10 years ago or have the values of our society changed?"

This study mirrors one that Harris Interactive took for the BSA in 1995. Thus, values of Americans young and old can be compared over a ten-year period. The earlier study sampled men and boys. The 2005 study included women and girls. Today, women make up approximately one-third of the volunteers in Boy Scouting. The Venturing program for older Scouts is coed with females representing a little less than half of its membership.

Harris surveyed randomly selected adults—1,524 in all. These surveys were done by telephone. The youth survey was conducted among 1,714 people under the age of eighteen. This was a survey conducted with students in public schools as well as parochial and non-parochial private schools.

Personal Satisfaction, but Worries about the Nation and the World

Harris Interactive found that American men and women (92 percent) are generally satisfied with their personal lives. Seventy-two percent say the same about their job or occupation. Satisfaction drops to 46 percent, however, when asked about the state of American society today. It drops further, to 38 percent, when asked about the state of the world today.

Youths surveyed also had a high level of satisfaction about their neighborhoods and schools (82 percent and 81 percent). They also felt safe in both, 82 percent and 88 percent, respectively. When it comes to the state of the world today, however, their satisfaction drops to 45 percent and their sense of safety goes down to 41 percent.

Clearly, worries about the uncertainties in the world are on the minds of both adults and youth.

Adult Values: Some Softer, Some Strong

Compared with men in the 1995 Harris survey for the BSA, "fewer men today place a high importance on showing concern for their neighbors' property, keeping their property clean and tidy, or attending religious services regularly." And fewer men, compared with the 1995 survey, think it is wrong under all circumstances to smoke marijuana; however, they are strongly opposed to the use of hard drugs such as heroin or LSD.

Eight out of every ten adults believe that having close family ties is essential to being happy. (It is highest—88 percent—with Hispanics).

Ninety-six percent say that children learn their values mostly from their parents. Nearly the same number, 95 percent, think parents should regulate what their children watch on television.

Eighty-five percent agree that attending religious services together as a family is important, and 62 percent agree strongly (with African Americans highest at 79 percent).

Ninety percent say that learning is a lifelong priority, and 72 percent say that saving for the future is one of their priorities.

Youth Values: Family Is Important

Like the adults surveyed, youth place great importance on family relationships. This is stronger with girls than with boys, but both say that "their parents are the most influential people when it comes to teaching values and ethics. "

Compared with the 1995 survey, fewer of those participating in the more recent one have been involved in cheating on homework or shoplifting and, surprisingly considering news reports, carrying a gun to school or joining a gang.

There is a widespread impression that youth are driven by peer pressure in their decisions about joining clubs and choosing extracurricular activities. This survey shows, however, that the opinions of parents/guardians weigh more heavily in these decisions (79 percent to 68 percent).

We hear much these days about a supposed lack of interest in reading on the part of young people, and that they get nearly all their information from television, computer screens, or text messages on cell phones. The facts don't align with that view, however. Eighty-nine percent of those surveyed like to read. Thirty-five percent like books; 33 percent prefer magazines; and only 12 percent favor comic books or book-length comics.

Only 6 percent never watch television; however, 36 percent watch it less than two hours a day. Another 27 percent watch it two to three hours a day; 13 percent report watching four to five hours; 6 percent six to seven hours; and 5 percent a whopping eight hours.

This is offset to a degree by their participation in activities. Sixty-eight percent go out for sports; 40 percent are involved in arts, music, dance, or drama; 33 percent in arts and crafts; 26 percent in hobbies; 24 percent in school clubs; 17 percent farming and gardening; 9 percent work on the school newspaper or yearbook; and only 9 percent are involved in none of these.

Of those who participate in organized after-school activities, 48 percent of the boys and girls surveyed participate in sports. Next comes the Boy Scouts (11 percent) followed by YMCA/YWCA, Girls Scouts, Big Brothers/Sisters, 4-H, Exploring (Boy Scout-related), Boys & Girls Clubs of America, Junior Achievement, Learning for Life, and Campfire USA.

Generally, today's young people feel good about themselves. They were asked if their skills in various areas were "excellent." Sixty-two percent rated themselves this way in their ability to make friends. Sixty-one percent said their skill in "having lots of friends" was excellent. Fifty-two percent said they excelled at being non-prejudiced. Forty-two percent ascribe excellence to "being self-confident," and the same number gave themselves that rating in "being a leader among my friends."

Their views on respecting older people and putting help for others ahead of self-interest mesh with Scout principles. Ninety-one percent said that older people should be respected, and 79 percent said helping others should trump self-interest.

Though I am imminently concerned about the deterioration of our culture and the influence it has upon our children, this survey shows at minimum that youth ideals are largely wholesome. The survey found large majorities supporting ideas that are widely considered to be tests of good citizenship. They were asked about the following list of traits, and whether they were "very or somewhat important to being a good American." The results are encouraging:

To show respect for your neighbor's property: 92 percent
To give time to help others: 91 percent
To give money to your church or religious organization: 75 percent
To attend church or religious services regularly: 74 percent
To keep one's room clean and tidy: 67 percent

The Influence of Scouting on Careers

Earlier, I listed statements of successful and famous men who attribute much of their success in life to the lessons they learned in Scouting. The Harris Interactive survey bears out these testimonies on a national scale.

Of the men Harris surveyed, 54 percent say they were in Scout programs in their youth, most as a Cub Scout or Boy Scout. On average, they were in Scouting for four years. A good-sized minority—42 percent—stayed in Scouting for five years or more.

Eighty-three percent of those who were in Scouting told interviewers that Scouting has been a positive influence on them. This is particularly true of the five-year-plus men. The former Scouts attribute the program with the positive development of character traits important to them. Below are the traits mentioned.

Traits	Percentage of Those Who Were in Scouts	Percentage of Those Who Were in Scouts Five or More Years
Being a good team player	84	96
Always being honest	84	96
Taking better care of the environment	84	95
Respecting the life and property of others	83	95
Having pride in your country	82	94
Respecting the elderly	82	94
Having confidence in your abilities	80	93

This conclusion is hard to escape: Scouting engenders respect for others, honesty, cooperation, self-confidence, and other desirable traits. And the longer one is in Scouting, the stronger the intensity of these character traits seems to grow.

The evidence increases as other traits are examined in the survey. Below are the percentages of respondents who say Scouting has positively influenced another set of traits.

Traits	Percentage of Those Who Were in Scouts	Percentage of Those Who Were in Scouts Five or More Years
Showing understanding to those less fortunate than yourself	78	91
Treating colleagues or coworkers with respect	76	88
Overcoming adversity or problems with courage	71	99
Avoiding the use of offensive language	61	75
Being successful in your career	60	83
Being responsible financially	59	73

The larger disparity between all who had Scouting experience and the five-years-or-more Scouts makes an argument for a boy staying with Scouting as he gets older.

Respondents also told the pollsters that Scouting had a positive effect on their "people" skills. Between 64 percent to 74 percent of total Scouts surveyed, and 75 percent to 88 percent of five-year-or-more Scouts, gave that assessment to such things as the ability to work with other people; family life while a Scout; the ability to accomplish tasks by yourself; the ability to accomplish tasks given to you by others; the ability to avoid difficulty with the law; school life while a Scout; and hobbies and other outside interests.

The benefits of Scouting have stuck with most of the men surveyed throughout their careers and lives. A range of 50 to 61 percent of total Scouts surveyed and 61 to 75 percent of the five-years-or-more Scouts said that Scouting has had a positive effect on them in these areas: ability to help others accomplish their goals; family life in later years; work life in later years; health and fitness; school life in later years; career development and advancement.

Scouts' Educational Attainment

As we have noted, the majority of adults surveyed by Harris were Scouts as boys. Their college and post-graduate degree attainment suggest again that Scouting had a positive influence on them.

The difference between Scouts and non-Scouts in high school is not great. Ninety-two percent of all Scouts graduated from high school. For five-years-or-more Scouts, it was 91 percent, and for non-Scouts, 87 percent.

It is in the college graduation rate that Scouts pull well ahead. Thirty-three percent of all Scouts graduated from college. Thirty-five percent of five-years-or-more Scouts did; however, only 19 percent of non-Scouts are college graduates. For post-graduate degrees, it is 10 percent, 10 percent, and 6 percent, respectively.

Family Life and Career

Although all the men surveyed were generally satisfied with their lives and their careers, the level of satisfaction was highest among former Scouts.

Very/Somewhat Satisfied

Your present life

All Scouts	94 percent
Five-years-or-more Scouts	97 percent
Non-Scouts	91 percent

Your job or occupation

All Scouts	77 percent
Five-years-or-more Scouts	83 percent
Non-Scouts	73 percent

Religious Participation

Former Scouts are active participants in the spiritual realm. Twenty-five percent attend services once a week, compared with 19 percent of non-Scouts. Total Scouts and five-years-or-more Scouts are ahead of non-Scouts in the more-than-once-a-week and two-to-three-times-a-month categories; however, non-Scouts lead in less-than-once-a-month attendance and "never attend religious services."

Ethics

All the men surveyed were asked whether a list of activities was "absolutely wrong under all circumstances." A majority of all Scouts, five-years-or-more Scouts, and non-Scouts agreed; however, total Scouts and five-years-or-more Scouts agreed in larger numbers than did non-Scouts in all five of the following categories: tossing out trash while driving; exaggerating one's education on a résumé; not declaring all income to the IRS; keeping excess change given at a store; taking pens or paper from the office for personal use.

"Good Citizenship" Issues

Respondents were shown a list of ten "good citizenship" responsibilities and asked which ones were "absolutely essential." In all categories, more former Scouts than non-Scouts agreed with this designation. The sharpest difference was in the category "vote in every election." Forty percent of all former Scouts agreed this was "absolutely essential," and a higher percentage, 47 percent of five-years-or-more Scouts, agreed; however, only 29 percent of non-Scouts agreed.

Scouting's Effect on Society

Former Scouts and non-Scouts agree emphatically that Scouting has a positive effect on society as a whole. From 89 percent (non-Scouts) to 99 percent (five-years-or-more Scouts), they say that Scouting helps character development. From 86 percent (non-Scouts) to 92 percent (five-years-or-more Scouts), they agree that Scouting is a real benefit to disadvantaged children in inner-city neighborhoods. "Scouting and good family are natural partners," agreed 78 percent of non-Scouts, 81 percent of all former Scouts, and 88 percent of former five-years-or-more Scouts.

How Scouting Affects the Behavior of Boys

The survey asked boys a group of questions separate from those asked the men. Several of these dealt with hypothetical situations designed to give pollsters an idea of how Scouting affects a boy's behavior.

Situation 1: "Your teacher arranges for students to visit a retirement home after school. Would you . . . ?"

	All Scouts	Five-year-plus Scouts	Non-Scouts
Choose to go home and do something else	21 percent	23 percent	30 percent
Tell your teacher you can go on the visit	49 percent	41 percent	34 percent
Tell your teacher you will think about it	30 percent	36 percent	35 percent

Situation 2: "Your best friend hangs out with people who do destructive things and he/she asks you to come with them. Would you . . . ?"

	All Scouts	Five-year-plus Scouts	Non-Scouts
Go with them and participate in their activities	15 percent	17 percent	14 percent
Go with them, but not participate	32 percent	23 percent	32 percent
Tell him/her you won't go with them	52 percent	61 percent	53 percent

Situation 3: "You see a classmate bring a gun to school. Would you . . . ?"

	All Scouts	Five-year-plus Scouts	Non-Scouts
Not say anything to anyone	8 percent	6 percent	14 percent
Tell your teacher or a parent	84 percent	83 percent	71 percent
Tell your friends but no one else	7 percent	9 percent	14 percent

Situation 4: "Your friend takes an apple from a stand without paying for it and gives it to you. Would you . . . ?"

	All Scouts	**Five-year-plus Scouts**	**Non-Scouts**
Eat the apple	11 percent	10 percent	18 percent
Take it back to the fruit stand	37 percent	33 percent	33 percent
Give it back to your friends and say you'd rather not eat it	52 percent	57 percent	48 percent

While boys not in Scouting scored well in answering these ethical questions, those in Scouting and especially those who have been in it five years or more scored much higher. It reinforces again the conclusion that Scouting has a positive effect on a boy's behavior and, in my view, the longer boys are exposed to Scouting's values, the more they are shaped by them.

Scouts on Character Building

Among the boys surveyed who are or have been Scouts, there is a high degree of agreement that Scouting has taught them traits that constitute good character.

The following are the percentages of those who agree that Scouting has taught them the traits listed:

To treat others with respect—80 percent
To have confidence in myself—80 percent
To take better care of the environment—79 percent
To get along with others—78 percent

To always give your best effort—78 percent
To set goals for myself—78 percent
To care for other people—78 percent
To be a leader—76 percent
To always be honest—75 percent
To respect adults—75 percent

The Scouts agreed that Scouting has helped their performance in specific areas, such as physical fitness (66 percent), science (56 percent), reading (52 percent), and math (50 percent).

Along with that, they report that Scouting has increased their interest in these important areas: emergency preparedness (78 percent), physical fitness (73 percent), engineering (69 percent), and the environment (69 percent). Also, Scouts who rated their skills as "excellent" in these four areas were well ahead, in percentages, of non-Scouts:

	All Scouts	Five-year-plus Scouts	Non-Scouts
Environment	33 percent	41 percent	22 percent
Emergency preparedness	41 percent	52 percent	36 percent
Physical fitness	54 percent	60 percent	52 percent
Engineering	39 percent	40 percent	35 percent

If evidence were ever needed that Scouting is a positive influence on boys, the Harris survey supplied it.

Taking Inventory of Society

Is American society going to hell in a hand basket? I was watching the 2007 U.S. Open Tennis Tournament, when the commentator pointed out how many young, up-and-coming female players are from Eastern Europe and the former Soviet Union. It wasn't a matter of merely bemoaning American tennis and the lack of stars besides the Williams sisters, because as he pointed out, very few of the up-and-coming players were from Western Europe either.

I began thinking about the tennis stars of the Cold War era. Sure, Martina Navratilova was of Czech origin, as was Ivan Lendl, but most stars came from the Western world—Billie Jean King, Chris Evert, Tracy Austin, Stefi Graf, John McEnroe, Bjorn Borg, Jimmy Connors, Mats Wilander, Stefan Edberg, Boris Becker, Pete Sampras and Andre Agassi. It's not that the Communists didn't care about sports. They could be downright dominating (swimming, gymnastics, and hockey come to mind) when they chose to focus on a particular sport, and prevent their best from turning pro. But what explains a post-Cold War explosion in tennis in countries liberated from the yoke of Communism?

I believe there is a hunger in those newly free societies that isn't as strong in the Western world because our bellies are full. If you live in Serbia, Romania, or Poland, it's nice to be free, but life may remain pretty strenuous. The chance to arise out of difficult circumstances is still rare. Tennis for Eastern European women seems like basketball for our inner-city kids over the last half century: a way out.

Are we so wealthy, so powerful, so blessed that we don't work as hard? And even if we don't, does it matter with the advantages we already have in the competitive world? Compared to Western Europeans, Americans can't be accused of taking it easy. We work much longer hours than our friends across the Atlantic. They have three-hour meals; we have fast food so we can cram as much into our day as possible. Their coffee breaks are for relaxation; ours are so we can infuse enough caffeine into our bloodstream to make us more productive in the late afternoon.

I am not one of those pessimists who only sees bad in our youngest generation. I see extraordinary young men and women who serve our country during times of war and make tremendous sacrifices. They are as brave as the bravest World War II heroes. I see young people going into teaching because of a love of learning and dispensing knowledge. I see young athletes who don't make public fools of themselves, but instead make a real impact in the locker room by leading their friends away from the path of ruin. There are many bright young people, but are they awash in a sea of dysfunction, self-indulgence, and greed? Are they but a virtuous minority in a chorus full of virtuosos?

Despite our great wealth and success as a society, have we been tranquilized by what money can buy, and fallen asleep on the throne of moral authority? In other words, are we as hungry as we once were? Will this century be looked back upon as the Chinese century, with America relegated to the twentieth-century role of Great Britain: a fading power whose global reach has been diminished?

I come back to the issue of hunger. Though the politics of division cause resentment toward some Hispanic immigrants, I see a population that is largely law-abiding, aspiring to be upwardly mobile, and hungry.

Many see a stable job and a source of income as a tremendous improvement over the life they once knew in another country. For some, a minimum wage job is not a dead end but a life raft—a step onto the ladder to success, even if just the first rung.

These immigrants are hungry. They long for an opportunity to provide a good life for their family, and they don't want to waste the one great opportunity they have been given in America. Because of that, most enrich our society. We are better off for what they bring to the table.

For a much larger slice of America, that was born here, that was never deprived and has never known want, the perspective can be quite different. They have come to expect certain creature comforts, and take for granted basic necessities that millions of people lack: food, water, shelter, and clothing. They have advantages of which many could never conceive. Because of this, they do not have the same hunger to succeed; they know not how deep the abyss can be.

A compelling e-mail that seems to have been circulated widely makes the case. If the world were reduced to a town of one hundred people, and you had a college degree, you would be the only one with that level of education. If you had spare change in your pocket, your income would exceed most of the citizenry. There is a world of misery outside our borders of which we cannot conceive, and to some extent, blight within our borders that would shock us if we ever saw it.

We Americans—by the tens of millions—live "air conditioned lives" that make us immune to the sweat required of so many others who build something from nothing. We know neither the pain of poverty nor the great joy of emerging from it. We have our stresses and anxieties—in fact, I believe we are living in the era of anxiety—but the things that occupy our minds are less likely to be whether we can pay for food this month, or not nearly as much as people in other countries.

We have a drug for every problem and a diagnosis for every psychosis. We don't have children with "ants in their pants"; we have children with "attention deficit disorder." That is not to minimalize such conditions. Lord knows, whether you call it a disorder or a "paddleable offense," I had it as a kid. The point is, we defend today behavior we wouldn't tolerate in past years, and we treat with drugs today behavior we would attempt to fix through either discipline or love in the past. Don't take my statement too far: some drugs are a godsend for conditions we never treated right before they were available. But some kids don't need coddling or drug therapy; they need attention and tough love.

We would be wise to think about the widely held notion that great empires do not fall because of enemies at their gates but because of enemies within. Ultimately, the Romans did fall to the barbarians at their gates, but not until they had decayed so much from within that they no longer had the capacity to exercise their might.

When my father was growing up, he did not have access to flush toilets, indoor plumbing, television, radio, or a family vehicle, but he did have what he needed: loving parents, access to an education, clothes, food, and a place in a closely knit community. When he went to war, he most certainly knew he might not come home. Such a fate befell his waist-gunner on a B-17. The way of life he fought for had nothing to do with modern conveniences and the luxuries of being American, and everything to do with the right of people to be free. Freedom wasn't about riches; it was about a way of life—one that could lead to riches, but more importantly, one that could lead to the pursuit of happiness.

If we believe our technology, firepower, and educational attainment will save us from licentiousness, godlessness, and undisciplined living, we bet on a losing proposition according to the history of civilization (Rome, Greece, and Babylon, to name a few). Sure, prior empires did not have access to weapons that could annihilate mankind from the face of the earth. But it won't take a military invasion to remove us from our perch atop the world: only our wandering into a moral wilderness of indifference.

Don't believe me? Think about our test scores. We routinely finish close to last in key subject areas when compared to the results of students from the other industrialized nations. Consider this: the top quarter of the Chinese school population is roughly the same number as the enrollment in all North American schools. They have as many bright students as we have students. India is not that far behind. If they continue to educate their students and send them to learn in American universities so that many can come back home and transform their national economies, we will continue to slip economically by comparison. As a nation, we are also in great monetary debt to the

Chinese. More and more, they control the purse strings. It's not that they don't have huge economic challenges—they do—nor is it that they will surpass us in terms of quality of life, wealth, or other indicators of prosperity in the near future, but it must be pointed out that the trend is going in the wrong direction.

What has made America prosperous is not our ability to mass-produce innovations at the lowest cost, but our ability to come up with the newest innovations that can transform the economy. We create the idea, and others mass-produce more cheaply. Look at our past and you can see that Americans were at the forefront in inventing the faster computer chip, the best weapons systems and military technology, the best infrastructure, and the list goes on. But our ability to innovate is directly tied to our ability to educate. We cannot continue on the course of educational mediocrity and at the same time expect uninhibited economic excellence.

Why does this matter in a book about the Boy Scouts? It matters because I believe developing within our children the desire to succeed, hand in hand with the economic competency ensured by a quality education, is the key to continuing our prosperity.

You cannot divorce values from knowledge and expect results. Ultimately, knowledge harnessed for self-indulgence instead of societal good leads to moral decay and ultimately economic decay.

I do not advocate state-sponsored morality in the most general sense, but I do argue for the protection of organizations and entities whose influence on American values have been profoundly positive. And I do argue that we continue to make the case to our fellow citizens about the virtue of making right choices, while recognizing in a free society people must ultimately have the prerogative to make wrong choices. We live in an era where people want to make wrong choices and not reap the consequences. They want to be able to choose to engage in unsafe sex and then be freed from the consequences, such as having a baby. They want to nurture their addictions to television and the Internet but not reap the consequences of becoming disconnected from their loved ones. They want to be able to indulge by imbibing alcohol, get behind the wheel, and hope there will not be consequences for their dangerous actions.

To teach freedom and individualism without teaching responsibility and social obligation is a recipe for disaster. To then turn around and defend as victims those who exercise freedom without responsibility is an outrage propagated by modern culture. We cannot lose sight of tough love and the incentive it creates for people to correct wrong behavior. Yes, these are judgment calls. Ask any judge at sentencing: is this person a chronic danger under the influence of alcohol, or did they have one bad night? And what is the proper punishment? Sometimes mercy says give a person a second chance. Sometimes it says you have had your chance. Or at least, that is what is merciful for the rest of society and the victims of crime.

The purpose of Boy Scouts and many other civic-minded organizations is not to instill perfection, but to help young people begin the relentless pursuit of good. We need organizations like this in a day and age when they are becoming the exception, not the rule.

To attack such organizations because they do not conform to a minority view about spiritual or lifestyle choices is to sacrifice the greater good for a narrow agenda. It is not as if the Boy Scouts teach intolerance toward the atheist or the homosexual; it is just not the purpose of the Scouts to engage in a debate about these issues. There are other forums for such discussions, and there is no need to make Scouts an experiment in social engineering.

In a wider context, it is also not my personal belief that society should condemn either the homosexual or the atheist. We must draw a line in the sand: people have the right to decide for themselves what they will believe in the core of their being, and how they will live. We can debate the wider social ramifications of how such belief and behavior impacts society, but ultimately freedom must prevail and people must be able to pursue the life they desire as long as it does not harm others. For those who want to throw stones at homosexuals in the name of calling out sin, may they be just as loud about adultery among heterosexuals and pornography among their own churchgoing friends.

We must approach these issues with humility no matter how strongly we feel about them—humility based on self-awareness and the recognition of our own sin. Doing otherwise is what gets those of us who identify with the Christian conservative movement in such hot, hypocritical water.

My conclusion: let us not be quiet about the culture, but at the same time, let us be loving toward those with whom we have deeply held disagreements and in doing so be humble at all times.

The Road Ahead: Can Scouting Survive?

The answer to that question is largely contingent on the outcome of the wider war. As I have stated throughout this book, the war on Scouting is just a microcosm of the left's multi-front attack on traditional American values. It is a contest of values and ideas between the proponents of secular humanism and the advocates of traditional values.

Secular humanism, at its core, elevates the individual to the center of the human drama. Truth is not bestowed upon us by a Creator, the humanists believe, but is determined by the individual, which is why we often call it moral relativism; it is relative to one's own viewpoint. The idea is that so many of the things we have traditionally called truth are now subject to individual interpretation. Some say there is no fixed "right" or "wrong," only different opinions.

If traditional society condemns the viewing of pornography as unhealthy because it objectifies women, reducing them to mere objects in order to fulfill one's desires, the secular humanist would retort that the individual has the right to view pornography, and whether it is healthy or not is a decision wholly to be made by that individual—regardless of its role in turning some viewers into eventual predators.

Secular humanism would make the truth of God's existence dependent on one's own view. They would say worship the God you choose, almost as a psychological construct by which you can perceive life and cope with it. In that scenario, what is true is less relevant than what enriches one's life based on what one perceives to be true. On its face, this is preposterous. Yes, it may have psychological benefits, but it does not speak to transcendent truths that are greater than, and in no way dependent upon, what an individual perceives. Either God exists or He doesn't, and this isn't relative to one's own perspective. In other words, it is true or false independent of man's perception. As Paul put it about Christian doctrine, either Jesus truly is the answer to sin—the Way, the Truth, and the Life as Christ says in John 14:6—or Christians "remain dead in their sins." Either faith in Christ can cleanse all people of their sin, or none, but not some (though indeed, it only does cleanse some, not because it isn't sufficient for all, but because the power of God's forgiveness is only appropriated by some). The truth of Christ's death, resurrection, and power over sin is absolute: it is either absolutely sufficient to cover all of mankind, or it absolutely covers none. What we believe about it does not determine its truthfulness.

C. S. Lewis advanced the idea about Jesus as the Christ that we are given only three choices about him: that he is either Lord, liar, or lunatic. Many—especially secular humanists—want to recognize Jesus as a good teacher, but nothing more. But why call him good if he has lied about his claims of deity and misled two millennia of followers? Then he could only be called a giant fraud. Once again, though, the truth is not something we meld to fit our own views; it is independent of it. The attempt to make Christ into merely a good teacher is an avoidance of the only three potential "truth options" that we have concerning him.

I believe secular humanism emanates out of man's great downfall: the sin of pride. To put God on the throne of our lives, to surrender to a Higher Being in complete submission, in the mind of the secular humanist, is to surrender credit for the accomplishments of one's life. It is essentially to say, "I am not so great because everything thing I have ever accomplished is a gift from God." To some, this is not an appealing notion. We want to be loved, we want to be famous, we want to be widely acclaimed as successful, and we want all this to be because we achieved it on our own. Yet, where does our capacity to think, dream, and emotionally connect come from? It is a gift present within our DNA. Sure, our talent can either be developed or not developed, but we can't claim credit for the potential with which we are born. This, by the way, is true even if there is no God (a notion I dispute) because our every gift emanates from the unique combination of the genes inherited from our parents.

The life of the secular humanist has a depressing end. Regardless of how great they may consider their accomplishments in life, or how much money they make, it is still the case that they have lived their life for a philosophy that elevates self instead of a worldview that elevates the Creator. All their possessions will be left behind, and the only thing that will matter is what God thinks of their life in the face of eternity. Shall they stand before God and brag that they fought to scrub His glorious name from the nation's pledge? Shall they seek His approval for attacking private organizations merely because these organizations proclaim His existence? Shall they cite their work defending those that deny His existence? Shall they proclaim that they successfully made the worship of self their own idol, in violation in one of the sacred Ten Commandments?

What we get when we worship self are billions of "gods" who determine on their own what is truth and what is to be valued. Contrast this to the notion that what is true and what is to be valued emanates from one being, God the Creator. Then take this one step further, and acknowledge that He not only is the author of truth, but has revealed truth to mankind. In *Mere Christianity*, Lewis has done a splendid job of illustrating how natural law is clearly written on our hearts in accordance with the values attributable to a loving God. I cannot begin to do justice to his brilliant argument, but can only commend one to read it. What I can say is I find it preferable to believe in truth that emanates from an all-knowing being than in the concept of "truth" espoused by several billion individual gods who have made a mess of the world they inhabit. If you believe in the secular humanist perspective, how do you reconcile so many shades of truth into a society that works? How do you prosecute the murderer if he believes he has a right to take the life of another and the right to determine his own morality, his own truth? Only by elevating the consensus view of a society can we do such, but how can it occur if truth is relative to the individual? Only when truth transcends the individual—greater than any one person's individual notions of right and wrong—can it truly govern our lives in a way that is good for the many.

Ironically, the secular humanist would impose the view of an individual on the many, violating their sacred individual rights as expressed through a large, private organization such as the Boy Scouts. This is not tolerance; this is insanity. It is the imposition of a new kind of tyranny—the tyranny of the minority.

Why do I expound so much on the mindset of the secular humanists? Because they want to force their moral precepts upon the wider society. They want to prohibit the Boy Scouts from requiring that all Scouts profess their belief in God. They want to undermine the moral underpinnings of the young minds that sit in their college classrooms, ridiculing the faith-based views they were taught as children by claiming that science and social science make such views a myth. They want to put religion in a box in order to proselytize for their own "religion," where man is his own god. They are a destructive force.

The proponents of suits attacking the Scouts' profession of belief in God, especially the American Civil Liberties Union, took the position that the Boy Scouts had no right to exclude people who refused to declare a "duty to God." Protecting the "rights" of atheists had long been an ACLU cause, played out in numerous efforts to drive all references to God from the public square.

This effort runs counter to the beliefs of the founders of the American republic. All of them were either active in their faiths or, at the very least, were Deists, believing in a "higher authority."

The dollar is loaded with symbolic and actual references to God (e.g., "In God We Trust"). The Declaration of Independence states that all are "endowed by their Creator with certain unalienable Rights." These facts hardly represent an endorsement of atheism.

The ACLU, however, takes the initial clause of the First Amendment to the U.S. Constitution—"Congress shall make no law respecting an establishment of religion, or prohibiting the free exercise thereof"—and emphasizes but one phrase, the first, in an effort to eliminate public references to God, thus making atheism co-equal. In ignoring the second phrase of the First Amendment, which precludes Congress from prohibiting the free exercise of religion, the ACLU claims Christmas decorations and Ten Commandments tablets in public parks are evidence that Congress has somehow "established" a state religion. In some cases they have won removal of the "offending" symbols by threats of lawsuits or actual suits.

They did not win in their effort to force the Boy Scouts to remove "duty to God" from the Scout oath. Approximately four million boys and men involved in Scouting every week have no difficulty reciting the Scout Oath because they believe in God. They realize that atheists are free to believe anything or nothing as they wish, but these individuals may not change the criteria for Scout membership. For that matter, they could if they wished to form a national atheist youth group.

Robert Rakkety, in a speech to the American Atheists National Convention in March 2005, referred to a passage in the *Boy Scout Handbook* that says, "Scouts should respect and defend the right(s) of all people." He says this makes them hypocrites for excluding atheists from membership. There is, however, no inconsistency here. The passage in the *Handbook* refers to defending others' rights. One can defend the right of another to speak out for atheism without agreeing with that person that, as an atheist, he should be admitted to membership in one's Scout troop.

Rakkety urged his listeners to join Scouting for All, a lobbying organization that seeks to bring pressure on Congress to withdraw the BSA's charter and to put pressure on the Scouts to change their membership criteria via letters to the editor and op-ed articles in newspapers.

Atheists and human secularists have not been shy in criticizing the Boy Scouts' defense of its "duty to God" phrase in the Scout Oath. In the *Secular Humanist Bulletin* (15/3 [4 December 2003]), Margaret Downey wrote, "BSA now joins the ranks of disgraceful private clubs that promote bigotry and prejudice. Ethical members of the BSA should be appalled to know that an organization to teach Scoutcraft is now promoting separatism and bigotry." Her criticism turned to attributing motives to the BSA that were not there: "My worst fears have been realized. Religious zealots have seized control of BSA and they will destroy all that has been good with their fear and loathing toward the non-religious community." Her comments followed the dismissal of a complaint she had brought to the Pennsylvania Human Rights Commission in 1999.

Over-the-top bloggers regularly bash the Boy Scouts. *Wonkette*, one with many followers on the political far left, wrote on April 6, 2007,

> The military-boy scout orgy known as 'Jamboree' will be held as planned behind the gates of Fort A.P. Hill in Virginia, the 7th Circuit Court of Appeals ruled Wednesday. Every four years, the boy scouts and soldiers get together for a no-holds-barred bash. ACLU communists said this was wrong because the boy scouts also have to pray to Jesus, so they shouldn't be using public property—which is kind of insane, considering that the entire federal government is run by god-nuts who spend all their time on public property muttering to god. Despite their prayers, the American god is not a big fan of the boy scouts or their vile jamboree. Last time they held it at Fort A.P. Hill, lightning killed four Scout leaders while more than 300 Scout kids collapsed in the heat after waiting for hours for a promised visit by President Bush. Scouts were struck by lightning at the 2001 jamboree, too. ("Jesus-Loving Boy Scouts Defeat ACLU!" 6 April 2007, wonkette.com/politics/foul-weather/ jesus+loving-boy-scouts-defeat-ACLU-250370.php.)

Over time, cases based on the "duty to God" were overtaken by those involving the BSA's policy that did not permit active homosexuals to serve as adult volunteers in Scout troops. This policy bears some similarity to the military's "don't ask, don't tell" policy. Routinely, prospective adult Scout leaders have not been asked about their sexual preferences. This was, and is, consistent with Scouting's belief that its program is about giving boys character-building activities, not sex education, which is the parents' responsibility.

Over time there have probably been a number of gay adult Scout leaders. If so, their preference has not been known because their sex lives have been a private matter. They have not discussed the subject any more than, say, a divorced father who is a Scout leader would be expected to discuss his dating patterns.

Openly active gays, particularly advocates, present a problem. Because gay activism is central to their lives, it would unavoidably be a topic of conversation within a Scout troop. This would distract from the mission of Scouting: character building, not sex education.

This does not mean the Scouting movement "hates" homosexuals or thinks their legal rights should be circumscribed in any way. It does mean, however, that Scouting does not want time and attention to be diverted from its mission. It believes that the presence of gay activists in its ranks would do that.

A gay activist or sympathizer might say Scouting's opposition to openly gay Scout leaders is discriminatory because of the controversial claim—one that is gospel in leftist circles—that gay people are "born that way." To argue with such a notion—which I have done in a previous chapter of this book—is to "oppose science." Have you ever noticed how the left commonly claims people of faith and positions of faith are diametrically opposed to science? "You believe in the Creation Story? Well that's fine in terms of your faith, but of course science has discounted the possibility." You can't have a rational discussion with the left about nature versus nurture, global warming, or the validity of evolution because they claim science has already weighed in. Yet, science reveals new discoveries all the time, and in so doing, for instance, makes the evolutionary explanation less plausible. If, however, someone makes an argument for intelligent design, we are told it should be taught in a class on faith. Here we are again at a well-worn crossroads: where the left advocates tolerance while crushing dissenting views.

When it comes to manmade global warming, many scientists who once advocated it is caused by human activity have abandoned that theory after closer study. Where are the stories on this growing *scientific* movement? Alas, many in the news media have already invested too much in a particular storyline, just as some scientists continue promoting It's-All-Our-Fault theory because their research grants are dependent on it. In twenty-five years, when this theory has been discarded alongside other ideas that didn't stand the test of time, perhaps there will be a one-day story announcing its demise. Then the left will be on to its next theory created to advance a particular political agenda.

The power of the news media is not necessarily that of shaping people's values, but shaping people's perspective on events and facts. When we bridged a $10 billion state budget gap in Texas with a combination of spending cuts and delayed payments, rather than the left's knee-jerk prescription of tax hikes, there wasn't one serious effort on the part of the media to examine the plight of the taxpayer in the face of higher taxes. There was, however, a seemingly endless array of stories about the human victims of spending cuts.

We read about impoverished AIDS victims who would die if the state no longer subsidized their expensive medicines. We read about children cut off the welfare and insurance rolls. We read about people with disabilities kicked out on the street. Yet, what about the family that must choose between paying its utility bills or putting gasoline in the car if we raise their taxes higher? What about the effect of higher taxes on those already paying higher insurance bills? What about the time lost with children for a parent who must work a second job because government can't control spending?

The message from the media on Scouting is to lionize the gay scoutmaster who was only "being honest" about his identity, and to highlight the harsh stand of Scouting with values stuck in the *Leave It to Beaver* era. You cannot have a serious discussion about the culture war without discussing the media that shape public perceptions the most.

Of course the secular news media cannot advocate a faith perspective, but they can refrain from expressing a bias that people of faith hold irrational views about issues that have scientific ramifications. They can also explore the *scientific* basis for theories such as intelligent design.

There *is* good news for the great many Americans who believe in the mission of the Boy Scouts and the millions more who believe in the values it instills in young men. For all the disdain shown by those of the left, they remain a minority because their ideas are not salient for most Americans. So far as the news media goes, it seems likely that there is a correlation between the anti-traditional-values bias often found there and the media's low public approval ratings. Poll after poll shows the media at about the approval level of used car salesman (and the latter, recognizing their credibility problem, now sell "pre-owned" cars).

Can Scouting survive this onslaught? Yes, as long as Scouting remains what it is and doesn't try to bend to the winds of political correctness. I asked this question of such notable Eagle Scouts as Robert Gates and E. Gordon Gee.

Incoming Ohio State President E. Gordon Gee made an interesting comparison to his life in the academic world: "I think Scouting will outlast you and me. As long as it focuses on its fundamentals and executes them well, while being modern in its approach, I think Scouting will still be here. Here's an example. In the early '90s many told me that bricks-and-mortar universities were going to disappear. The Internet would take over. We would have 'virtual' universities. Yet, if anything, traditional universities have become more powerful than ever because they have adapted to the changing environment. And that is what I think will happen with Scouting."

I asked Defense Secretary Gates if he thinks Scouting has the impact today that it had on youth in, say, the 1940s, '50s, and '60s. He made this interesting observation: Seven or eight years ago the Scouts starting breaking records for the number of Scouts achieving the highest rank, Eagle, each year. As to whether Scouting can survive the onslaught of the left, he said, "In terms of its major contributions, I hope it is exactly where it is today. That is, outside of religion, it is the foremost vehicle for teaching young men about values and the importance of character. Those values remaining unchanging, whether the year is 2007 or 2037."

I believe Scouting will survive as long as it sticks to the virtues and values of the great middle class. I believe, too, that Scouting will survive if those values of the middle class are not replaced by a culture of licentiousness. Not all people will live up to the highest standards of personal conduct. People make mistakes. They may become intimately involved in wrong relationships before they are intellectually or emotionally mature. They may turn to food or alcohol to ease pain and soothe a latent desire for significance. Sometimes they think they would rather be entertained than enlightened. Nevertheless, what they wish for their children is not what the radical left began preaching in the 1960s. They do not want their children to live in bondage to sexual addiction or die from sexually transmitted diseases. They desire with all their hearts that these children avoid illegal narcotics and the consuming narcissism to which they can lead. They don't expect "choir boys," but they won't tolerate their own children shoplifting or cheating on tests.

For the great middle class, there is a lot more than a morass of gray—there is a lot of black and white, of right and wrong. And when they look at the Boy Scouts, they see an organization that affirms their views; an organization that urges young men to be kind, to live by a code of decency, and to be honest. They see a group that espouses the American value of service, the important trait of trustworthiness, and the enriching quality of perseverance. They recognize, as signified by the uniform worn by troop members, that the Scouts teach that the whole is greater than the individual, and that the best way for individuals to develop is to do so within the context of community.

These are values worth fighting for and ideas to live by. This has been so since the foundation of the republic, and will be so long as young men are exposed to the lessons and lifelong values taught by the Boy Scouts.

Afterword

If you feel compelled to help the Boy Scouts of America withstand the withering legal assault, there is a way you can help. Please give generously to: Legal Defense, Boy Scouts of America, National Council, P.O. Box 152079, Irving, Texas 75015-2079.

In this book I couldn't begin to do justice to the number of heroes that have risen through the ranks of the Scouts. If you want to share your own stories, please submit them to the website I have created for this project: www.onmyhonorthebook.com. Or, if you want to share information about Scout scholarship opportunities not contained in this book, or the latest horror stories about culture warriors attacking the Scouts, I would love to hear your comments on the site. Join me in this important fight. Scouting needs you.

Appendix:
Scholarships for Scouts

Many people have asked me what scholarship opportunities exist for young men who have advanced through the ranks of Scouting. It turns out there is a plethora of colleges and universities seeking to attract Scouts—particularly Eagle Scouts—to attend their institutions. The following is a long list of such opportunities that exist, including ways to find out more information. This is not an exhaustive list, but merely what we could confirm at the time we went to publication. This shows, in one more way, that there is a tangible benefit to a young man sticking with Scouting.

Albright College
P.O. Box 15234
Reading, PA 19612-5234
An unlimited number of annually renewable $500 scholarships are available, regardless of Scouting rank.

American Humanics, Inc.
4601 Madison Avenue - Suite B
Kansas City, MO 64112
Dwight Thompson Scholarships
For Scouts seeking careers as professionals with youth or human service agencies
Award amount: Not shown
Web site:
http://www.humanics.org/site/c.omL2KiN4LvH/b.1098773/k.BE7C/Home.htm

American Legion
P.O. Box 1055
Indianapolis, IN 46206
American Legion Eagle Scout of the Year Awards

For Eagle Scouts
Award amounts: Winner, $10,000; three runners-up, $2,500 each
Web site:
http://www.legion.org/?secton=prog.evt.&subsecton=evt.scoutng&
content=evt._eaglescout

American Legion, Department of Tennessee
Eagle Scout of the Year
Award amount: $1,500 plus competition for $14,500 American Legion
National scholarship
Contact: Darlene Burgess, 615-254-0568
Web site: http:/www.tennesseelegion.org/youthprograms.shtml

Ave Maria University
Naples, FL
Eagle Scout Scholarship
Awarded to Eagle Scouts who meet the criteria for admission; must maintain a GPA of 3.0 or higher when enrolled.
Award amount: Each award covers half the cost ($9,000) of annual tuition.
Web site: www.avemaria.edu/scholarships/#Eagle%20Scout%20Scholarship

Birmingham-Southern College
900 Arkadelphia Road
Birmingham, AL 35254
Eagle Scout Scholarships
For entering first-year students who are Eagle Scouts.
Award amount: $2,500 (renewable)
Web site: http://www.bsc.edu/academics/catalog/catalog2003-
04/pages/admission/scholarships.htm

Cape Fear, NC, Council, BSA
P.O. Box 7156
Wilmington, NC 28406
Betty & Ellis Tinsley, Sr., Eagle Scout Scholarship Fund
For Eagle Scouts
Award amount: $1,200
Web site: http://www.capefearcouncilbsa.org/scholarship.htm

Cascade Pacific Council, BSA

2145 S.W. Naito Parkway

Portland, OR 97201

CPC Eagle Scout Association College Scholarships

For Eagle Scouts in the Cascade Pacific Council who have distinguished themselves.

Award amount: $2,500 plus four $500 scholarships for runners-up

Royden M. Bodley Eagle Scout Scholarship

For Eagle Scouts in the Cascade Pacific Council who are interested in pursuing education in wildlife conservation, forestry, or allied subjects in educational institutions located in Oregon.

Award amount: varies

Web site: http://www.cpcbsa.org/advancement/scholarships/generalscholarships/cpcesa/index.html

Columbia College

1001 & Rogers

Columbia, MO 65216

Offers a $500 scholarship to an Eagle Scout or Explorer admitted to the college.

Doane College

Admissions Office

1014 Boswell

Crete, NE 68333-2430 (1-800-333-6263)

Zenon C.R. Hansen Leadership Scholarship

For Eagle Scouts

Award amount: $7,000 annually; possible renewal

Dowling College

Director of Financial Aid

Oakdale, NY 11769 (516-244-3110)

Nathaniel M. Giffen Memorial Endowed Scholarship

A $2,000 four-year scholarship awarded annually to two freshmen who have demonstrated a strong background in Scouting.

Drury College
900 North Benton Avenue
Springfield, MO 65802
Lawrence and Helen Lynch Endowed Eagle Scout Scholarship
Award amount: $2,000
Web site: http://www.drury.edu.

Eagle Scout Scholarships
Eagle Scout Service, S220
Boy Scouts of America
P.O. Box 152079
Irving, TX 75015-2079
Eagle Scout Academic Scholarships
Award amount: Not specified
Web site: http://www.nesa.org/scholarships/58-714.pdf

Hall/McElwain Merit Scholarships Award
Award amount: Not specified
Web site: http:/www.nesa.org/scholarships/58-714.pdf
Scholarship application forms:
Web site: http://www.nesa.org/scholarships/index.html

Federal Criminal Investigators' Service Award
National Law Enforcement Scholarships & Awards
P.O. Box 152079
Irving, TX 75015-2079
For Law Enforcement Explorers
Award amount: U.S. savings bond

Grand Canyon University
Scholarship Coordinator
3300 West Camelback Road
Phoenix, AZ 85017

Presidential Leadership Eagle Åward
For students who are Eagle Scouts
Award amount: $300 renewable annually

Green Mountain College
One College Circle
Poultney, VT 05764
Make-a-Difference Scholarships
Awarded to people who have made a difference in the life of another person
and/or their community and wish to continue their education.
Award amount: Winners are awarded full tuition, room, board, and fees for
up to four years.
Web site: http://admissions.greenmtn.edu/tuition_aid/makeadifference.asp

Gulf Ridge Council Chapter
Eagle Scout Scholarship Application
13228 N. Central Avenue
Tampa, FL 33612
Gulf Ridge Eagle Scout Scholarship
Award amount: $500 non-renewable. For currently registered Eagle Scouts,
graduating high school seniors or college freshmen
Web site:
http://www.boyScouting.com/documents/EagleScholarshipApplication_00
0.pdf

Illinois American Legion Scholarship Program
Legion Scout Chairman
The American Legion
P.O. Box 2910
Bloomington, IL 61702
Boy Scout Scholarship
Awarded annually. Students must be graduating high school seniors and
qualified Senior Boy Scouts or Explorers and residents of Illinois.
Award amount: $1,000 to winner; four $200 runner-up awards
Web site: http://illegion.org/scholarship.html

International Association of Fire Chiefs Explorer Scholarship
Learning for Life, S210
P.O. Box 152079
Irving, TX 75015-2079
For Fire Service Explorers
Award amount: $500 (each, two awards)
Web site: http://www.learningforlife.org/exploring/scholarships/pdf/iafcf.pdf

Johnny "MO" & Ann Nassour Scouting Scholarship
P.O. Box 820425
Vicksburg, MS 39182-0425
Eligibility: Active Scouts in Vicksburg or Warren County, Mississippi
Award amount: Not specific
Web site: http://www.bsatroop7.org/scholorship.pdf

Johnson & Wales University
8 Abbot Park Place
Providence, RI 02903
Gaebe Eagle Scout Scholarship
Award amount: $1,000
Web site: http:/www.jwu.edu/admiss/scholarships/index.htm

Lamar University
4400 MLK Boulevard
P.O. Box 10009
Beaumont, TX 77710
Don M. Lyle Regents Scholarship
Award amount: Varies

Lambuth University
Office of Scholarships & Financial Aid
Lambuth Blvd.
Jackson, TN 38301 (901-425-3330)
Leadership Scholarship
Open to Eagle Scouts
Award amount: $800 annually for four years

Law Enforcement Scholarships & Awards

P.O. Box 152079
Irving, TX 75015-2079
Sheryl A. Horak Law Enforcement Explorer Memorial Scholarship
For Law Enforcement Explorers
Award amount: $1,000 (one-time scholarship)

Lindenwood University

209 S. Kingshighway
St. Charles, MO 63301
Scout Youth of the Year Award
Award amount: $11,200 scholarship plus $1,800 Work & Lean award,
renewable up to four years

Eagle Award/Venturing Silver Award
Award amount: $6,000 plus $1,800, renewable up to four years

Web site: http://www.lindenwood.edu

Local Scholarships

Library for Life
Lists local scholarships of many types in alphabetical order.
Web site:
http://www.libraryforlife.org/subjectguides/index.php/Local_Scholarships

Long Island University - C.W. Post Campus

Office of Enrollment Services - Room 210
Eagle Scout Scholarship Committee
720 Northern Boulevard
Brookville, NY 11548-1300
C.W. Post Eagle School Scholarship Program
Awarded annually to one Eagle Scout who is an entering full-time freshman
at LIU.
Award amount: $2,000
Web site:
http://www.cwpost.liu.edu/cwis/cwp/finaid/fall/applications/EAGLE%20S
COUT.pdf

McDaniel College
#2 College Hill
Westminster, MD 21157
Eagle Scout/Gold Awards
Award amounts: $2,000 (renewable)
Web site:
http://www.mcdaniel.edu/810.htm#McDaniel_College_Scholarships_and_
Grants

Mississippi State University
Office of Admissions & Scholarships
P.O. Box 6334
Mississippi State, MS 39762-6334
Gold Award/Eagle Scout Scholarship
For Mississippi Eagle Scouts
Award amount: $4,000
Web site:
http://www.admissions.msstate.edu/scholarships/additional.php#gold

Missouri Valley College
500 E. College
Marshall, MO 65340
American Humanics Scholarships
For Boy Scouts and members of other recognized youth groups.
Award amount: $5,000 yearly
Web site: http://www.moval.edu/admissions/finaid/scholarships.asp

National Catholic Committee on Scouting
NCCS - Emmett J. Doerr Scholarship
P.O. Box 152079
Irving, TX, 75017-2079
Emmett J. Doerr Memorial Distinguished Scout Scholarship
For Scouts who are practicing Catholics
Award amount: Three independent awards, each $1,000-$2,500
Web site: http:/www.nccs-bsa.org/business/EJDscholarship.php

National Jewish Committee on Scouting

S226, BSA
1325 West Walnut Hill Lane (P.O. Box 152079)
Irving, TX 75015-2079
Eagle Scholarship Programs
Chestier M. Vernon Memorial Eagle Scout Scholarship Program
Award amount: $1,000 annually for four years

Florence and Marvan Arkans Eagle Scout Scholarship Program
Award amount: $1,000 one time

Frank L. Weil Memorial Eagle Scout Scholarship Program

Award amount: $1,000 one time; two second-place scholarships for $500 each
Web site: http://www.jewishScouting.org

National Order of the Arrow Committee

National Office, BSA, Order of the Arrow
P.O. Box 152079
Irving, TX 75015-2079
E. Umer Goodman Scholarship Program
For OA members wishing to pursue a professional career in Scouting
Award amount: Not specified
Web site: http://www.main.oa-bsa.org/resources/forms/eugschol.pdf

National Technical Investigators

National Law Enforcement Scholarships & Awards
P.O. Box 152079
Irving, TX 75015-2079
Captain James J. Regan Memorial Scholarship
Award amount: $500 (each, two awards)
Web site:
http://www.learningforlife.org/exploring/scholarships/pdf/regan.pdf

New Mexico Military Institute
101 W. College Blvd.
Roswell, NM 88201-5173
Eagle Scout Scholarship
Award amount: Not specified
Web site: http:/www.nmmi.edu/FinancialAid/scholarshiplisting.htm

Occoneechee Council, BSA
P.O. Box 41229
Raleigh, NC 27629-1229
John William Pope Family Eagle Scout Scholarship
For Eagle Scouts in a troop within the Occoneechee Council territory
Award amount: Not specified
Web site: http://www.campdurant.com/Forms/jwp_scholarship_2006.pdf

Northern Star Council, BSA
Hulings Scout Service Center
393 Marshall Ave.
Saint Paul, MN 55102
Eagle Scout Scholarships
Award amount: More than 30 $1,000 scholarships awarded annually
Web site: http:/www.northernstarbsa.org/AdvancementAwards/Scholarships

Ohio Sate Fair
717 East 17th Ave.
Columbus, OH 43211
The Governor James A. Rhodes Junior Fair Endowment Fund Scholarship
Annual awards. For junior fair exhibitors who will be incoming freshmen or
undergraduate students at the Ohio State University College of Food,
Agricultural and Environmental Sciences.
Award amount: $1,000

Olivet College
Office of Admissions
320 S. Main Street
Olivet, MI 49076

Various scholarships
Award amounts: Varied
Web site: http://www.olivetcollege.edu/new_students/scholarships.php

Philadelphia Foundation
1234 Market Street - Suite 1800
Philadelphia, PA 19107
Mervyn Slutzer, Jr. Scholarship Fund
For Eagle Scouts
Award amount: $1,000 (renewable annually
Web site: http:/www.philafound.org/page33313.cfm

Pioneer Path Council, BSA
c/o Scout Executive
12 Mount Pleasant Turnpike
Denville, NJ 07834
Frank D. Visceglia Memorial Scholarship
Award amount: $1,000
Sponsored by the National Association of Industrial and Office Parks and
the Association for Commercial Real Estate
Web site: http://advancement.ppbsa.org/pdf/advf04.pdf

Point Park University
201 Wood Street
Pittsburgh, PA 15222
Scouting Award
For Eagle Scouts
Award amount: $1,000 annually
Web site: http://www.pointpark.edu

Tennessee Society of the Sons of the American Revolution
Contact: Stage Eagle Scout Chairman, Douglas Fidler
4033 Cave Mill Rd.
Maryville, TN 37922-3438
Scobey Rogers Eagle Scout Scholarship Program
Award amount: $500
Web site: http:/www.sar.org/tnssar/tneagle.htm

Troop 55

2328 North Blvd.
Houston, TX 77098
Troop 55 Eagle Scout Scholarship
Award amount: one-time award of $500
Web site: http://www.troop55.org/eaglescouts/scholarship/Default.htm

Scouts Canada Foundation

1345 Baseline Road
Ottawa, ON K2C 0A7
CANADA
Reginald K. Groome Memorial Scholarship
Award amount: Not specified
Web site: http:/www.scouts.ca/media//documents/rkgroomeform.pdf

Sea Scouts

National Sea Scouting Committee, BSA
P.O. Box 152079
Irving, TX 75105-2079
William M. Minto Memorial Scholarship for Sea Scouts
For Sea Scouts intending to attend the Sea Program at Texas A&M
University, Galveston.
Award amount: (approx.) $2,619 for Texas resident; $3,897 for out-of-state
residents
Web site: http:/www.seascout.org/reference/opportunities/minto.pdf

Sigma Phi Epsilon

Balanced Man Scholarship
National college fraternity offers scholarship through many of its 150 chap-
ters. Applicants need not be members. Amounts vary.
Web site: http://www.sigep.org/scholarship/default.asp

Springfield College

Director of Financial Aid
Springfield College
Springfield, MA 01109

Mortimer L. Schiff Scholarship Endowment Fund
To "an outstanding Scout who wishes to train for professional leadership in boys' work at Springfield College."
Award amount: $600 annually, renewable

Texas A&M University
Office of the Recruiting Coordinator
Corps of Cadets
Call: 1-800-TAMU-AGS
Scholarships for Scouts
For Eagle Scouts
Award amount: $500 per semester for the first four semesters

Trail's End Scholarship Program
9850 Westpoint Drive - Suite 100
Indianapolis, IN 46256
Eligible: Registered members of BSA. Must have sold a minimum of $2,500 (retail) Trail's End popcorn in a given period. Scholarships based on a percentage of sales.
Web site: http://www.coronadoscout.org/pubs/c/2_scholarshipform.pdf

United States Bureau of Alcohol, Tobacco and Explosives (Retirees' Association)
National Law Enforcement Exploring, S310
P.O. Box 152079
Irving, TX 75015-2039
AFTAR Scholarships
For Law Enforcement Explorers
Award amount: $1,000
Web site: http://www.learningforlife.org/exploring/scholarships/pdf/atf.pdf

United States Secret Service
Floyd Boring Award
Scholarships presented annually to Law Enforcement Explorers "whose achievements reflect the high degree of motivation, commitment and community concern that epitomizes the law enforcement profession."
Award amount: Two scholarships of $2,000 each
Web site: http:/www.learning-for-life.org/cgi/catalog/ catalog.cgi?p=web45&c=5

Index